To Hold in My Hand

To Hold in My Hand

Selected Poems, 1955–1983

Hilda Morley

With a Note by
Stanley Kunitz

The Sheep Meadow Press
New York City

Typesetting by Keystrokes, Lenox, Mass.
Printed in the United States of America

The Sheep Meadow Press, New York, N.Y.

Distributed by Persea Books
225 Lafayette St., New York, N.Y. 10012

Library of Congress Catalog Card Number: 83-40199

Library of Congress Cataloging in Publication Data

Morley, Hilda.
    To hold in my hand.

    I. Title.
PS3563.087187T6   1983   811'.54   83-40199
ISBN 0-935296-46-8
ISBN 0-935296-49-2 (pbk.)

ACKNOWLEDGMENTS

Grateful acknowledgment is made to the editors of the following publications in which these poems have appeared:

American Poetry Review, Black Mountain Review, Chelsea Review, Chicago Review, Endymion, Harper's Magazine, Heresies, The Hudson Review, Ironwood, Mail, Menomonie Review, Mother Jones, The Nation, New Directions 27, New Letters, Pequod, Sailing the Road Clear, Seneca Review and *Trellis.*

"Five Poems": "You standing always on a/," "That I raged up and down tonight/," "The hand of the unknown/," "That special hell of Dante's into/," "Why does the wild cherry tree/," "Stefan: His Birthday," "Poem: Here the sun, violet/," "Poem: Finding the names of birds here/," and "That Could Assuage Us" first appeared in *The Hudson Review.* They appear in this publication under the titles "Season," "Desert," "Webs," "Observed," "The Wild Cherry Tree," "Stefan: His Birthday," "Provence," "Conjuring," and "My Dear."

Mr. Kunitz's prefatory note is adapted from an essay that first appeared in *Ironwood* 20.

I am grateful to the Corporation of Yaddo, the MacDowell Colony and the Ossabaw Island Project for their hospitality during periods of residence when some of these poems were written.

for Denise

Contents

Prefatory note by Stanley Kunitz

Sea Lily

Makers

Faces of the City

To Love is to See

Darker

Steps on the Road

"Clair Bones"

Beginning Again

Where Joy Is

When I first met Hilda Morley, some twenty-five years ago, I had never read a poem of hers, and though we became good friends almost immediately, she was so unaggressive about her work that I remained largely in ignorance of it for almost a decade. I suppose she felt that there was room for only one genius in the family, and that one had to be her husband, the avant-garde composer Stefan Wolpe, a magnificently bright, rare, and ebullient spirit. Ever since their marriage in '48, she had given herself, not without a struggle, to the advancement of his difficult career. His death in '72 was a devastating blow, but at the same time it liberated her. The poems that she has written since then are born of an obsessive grief, a terrible loneliness, but at the same time they are celebrative, almost ritually so, steeped in the wine of what Donne called "the ecstasy." She is a poet of love more than she is a poet of loss, and she is a romantic as much as she is a metaphysician. Her newest poems, these outpourings of her late maturity, have an amazingly youthful ardor. They come to us wild and fresh. "Where something is being made is/where joy is," she writes. That joy of invention is inseparable from her word-play. Her poems seem to happen, not to be composed—a lovely illusion. We get the feeling that it is still, for her, rehearsal-time.

In the Fifties at Black Mountain, where Stefan taught for four years, Hilda Morley fell into the company of poets who could argue vehemently and long about problems of style. From Charles Olson in particular she learned something about the importance of spacing and breath unit and line-break, though her prosody in its eventual development is much more delicate and wavering than his, much less emphatic in its stressing. She prefers to slip tentatively into a poem, not to open with a flourish. Her characteristic line breathes naturally and is not conspicuously self-important, tending to fall to a weak syllable rather than rise to a strong one. She avoids heaviness of sound or sense, for her ear is tuned to a light and mobile syntax and is exquisitely sensitive to modulations of pitch and pace. Falling rhythm and skipping-stone technique contribute to an approximation of what she terms "this darting swooping movement of the mind." Often what we hear is the music of memory flowing through her lines:

                    There was a little
trail of notes you left to meet me
when I came back from teaching
                              & they said: Be welcomed
to our spaces   my sweet lady
                         & a flower
on the table saying: Flower-woman
                              & a shell more beautiful
than most that said:
                         Listen   Listen
to your own sea

    In the poem from which that passage is taken she meditates on John Donne's "Goodfriday, Riding Westward" and mounts on that meditation an oceanic spate of images pertaining to the death of her beloved—a montage with a span of three centuries, so rich and eloquent, even in its extravagance, that it constitutes a daring tour de force. It is a vehicle that threatens on almost every page to fall apart, but in the end, out of the "clair bones" and the dark years, the imagination seems to spread its sails and fly, ever westward, to the open water.

    During her Black Mountain days, Hilda Morley wrote a poem entitled "Goethe in Italy," in which she noted her protagonists's desire "to fix himself, to be anchored/ in the day's doing." She too is a traveler (not least of all, a mental

traveler) with an equal need for anchorage. Perhaps the
piece that most fully consolidates her supple powers is "That
Bright Grey Eye," a poem that luxuriates in her love of
landscape, her affinity with the great colorists among the
painters, particularly Turner, whose eye was as brilliant as
a child's and "who grew his thumbnail/ in the shape of an
eagle's claw"—the kind of fastidious detail this poet delights
in. At the poem's opening, it is early evening in late August
on Bank Street in Manhattan, her neighborhood, with the
light streaming on the Hudson from the sunset sky. That
sky of grey, in a chromatic scale of hues, blends into the
skies of Venice, evoking thoughts of Guardi and Turner,
and then of that town in Yorkshire where Turner first drew
mountain-landscapes, and then of certain lines of Blake
coincidentally associated by the author with that town: "And
when thou seest/ an Eagle, thou seest a portion of genius."
And suddenly, in a shifting of the light, it is Manhattan
again, at the corner of Bank Street and Bethune. The sky,
the river are afire. On the pavement the light trembles.
Everything prepares us for a crisis of transfiguration. But
Hilda Morley's masterful stroke is to delay that event, to
prevent it from happening too facilely. No eagles here. On
that most mundane of stages, the floor of a supermarket,
anchored with her "in the day's doing," we watch the unfold-
ing of a pathetic little drama that resolves in an act of ordi-
nary human kindness. And at last all the threads of the
poem are ready to be tied together, all its lights are ready
to flame as one:

> Then I breathe freely,
for yes, she is helpful, yes, she is
kind.
>   Outside on
the pavement, the light pouring itself away

is the light in the eagle's
eye   (or the eye of
a child)
                 (I saw it in a man's eye once:
                 but he's dead now more than
                 four years)
Drawing heat out of
surfaces,
        the light is
without calculation,
                is a munificence now,
is justified.

    Except for two recent small-press items, the bulk of
Hilda Morley's work has remained in manuscript or avail-
able only in a scattering of mostly esoteric periodicals. Yet
here she is in full stride, at an age when most lyric poets
have already quenched their song, undaunted by the years
of silence and neglect, having defended her pride and nur-
tured her gifts. It seems only fitting that Hilda Morley
should be the first recipient of the Capricorn Award, given
to a poet over forty in belated recognition of excellence.

STANLEY KUNITZ

Sea Lily

        Inside the sea-lily light
stirs
    a vibration.
          The pulse
of water nourishing the flower
                   outward
it moves fluting
the petals upward
           A shudder
of impulse   shaking
it into a cup,
       a cup
of fullness
        taking
from whatever passes
              giving
itself away

EILAT, ISRAEL, 1969

Makers

Psalm
for Denise

That I might go on the hunt
again
in the forest
with Artemis-Hecate,
or on
my own,
knowing that I am guided
by a dog-companion,
that I need have
no fear,
that the bird of the long
neck and wide-open
glance is with me
and looking
toward me

NEW YORK, 1960

There's No Mistake
for Meredith Luyten

To live by contraries   said Yeats
For me, the contraries of living
by reason   but not only
reason
          Believing in Joan of Arc, for one, but not in
the literalness of her visions,
                              believing
in her habit of saying "there's no mistake,"
                                   more in the power
of the beech-tree she dressed with the youth of Domrémy,
garlanded with flowers, more in the power of the nuts,
                                        the hardboiled
eggs, the celebration
of the little rolls they ate together, dancing
until nightfall;
                  better to believe
in the way Joan cut her hair like a page-boy,
                                   soup-bowl fashion,
more in her innocence
and in her love of the voices which she heard in the bells
at matins & at compline
                         so she promised the sexton
                         her fresh-baked cakes lest he
                         forget to ring them
I believe in the "poor red gown" she wore for meeting
her dauphin,
                  & the dark-green
                  robe, the color
                  of feuille-morte embroidered
                  with nettles—to mark the ruin
                  of France, which made her seem a herald
                  & an angel

4

& in her love of beautiful
clothes, even to the cloth-of-gold & the shoe
                                    "laced on the
outside of the foot" & beautiful
horses
        & in her courage, her confidence,
her boldness
            "For like those who walk in their
            sleep, she was calm in the face of
            obstacles, yet quietly
            persistent,"
choosing as patron-saint, Saint Catherine,
                                    guardian
of prisoners, the patron of getaways

            And I believe also
in her terror of death, her despair at being betrayed

            I live in
contradictions also without knowing
either who or often what I am,
                            remembering
of my ancestors that they loved the marvellous
& by extreme good fortune
saved from ignorance daily
only because I find it everywhere

                            THE MACDOWELL COLONY, 1972

5

The Wild Cherry Tree

Why does the wild cherry tree
                    blooming
on the Hudson
                make everything
more so
        more itself?
                    So the green
of the elm is greener than
when it stands alone,
                    the sky
bluer
    So you
are one of those
who make others
more themselves
                more what they
are!
    Of those who draw them to the extreme
verge,
        the edge
that crackles:
                that is
your beauty;
                that is what
you do

NEW YORK, 1960

Sow-Goddess

A whiteness behind me,
                    stronger
than light can be,
                    rises & makes me
unable to shift on the bed,
                    half-waking,
half-dreaming,
                    unable to
think or to stop my thinking,
                              unable
fully to dream,
                    I lie in a fever
of tossing
          & the moon bathes me,
my bones consumed by that fierceness,
my flesh parted by her hunger
                              Sow-goddess, mother
                              of my own whiteness
                              who shudders
                              into strength around me
how long is it
                    since I called on you,
in my longing, ancient mother of shells,
                              how long since I
turned to you,
              knowing you
mistress of my tides in this solstice,
this shortest
of all nights in the year,
                    watcher
of paths & fountains,
                    whose eyes bear witness

to the currents of my abeyance,
in the skein of
your powers
hold me

NEW YORK, 1974

Narcissus in Georgia

The narcissus belongs to
Persephone,
       so it was
said by the Greeks
          Only
now,
    in March,   even
here,   in Georgia,
            does it
open itself freely
to the warm air,
        showing
six pure-white petals
        at last,
starlike—head thrown backward
in whiteness:
       taking
its fate in its hands
        after being
buried in darkness,
        certain
of showing its face most beautifully
this once   after winter,
          bestowing
itself in assurance
for this.
    That hiding
all winter was worth it—
to offer such grace,
        such whiteness,
awareness of being vulnerable—
faintness of its perfume.

OSSABAW ISLAND, GEORGIA, 1975

9

Still-Life
for John Blee

Outside, November,
                    the cold blowing
in our faces, walking
down Madison—
                    inside the little building,
watercolors, the late ones, by Cézanne
                    We stand in front of
one, on the back wall: the flask, the apples
                              a bottle
& glasses with the light on them,
                                        liquid
in the bottle
                    Everything that's luminous
& soaring moves,
                    moves upward
there & blows us with it
                              All that is physical
& weighted,   or might be
subject to decay
                    turns into
a vapor, a cloud,
                    an energy
of movement, of light in itself,
                                   but vapor
that's solid,
              cloud that's tangible,
light that's substance
                    & I say—Praise,
praise is what it is, making
the apples, the flask, the bottle
& the wall behind them soaring
& full & luminous at once,
                              filling

10

the spaces in our body with movement
& light,   no single
interstice untouched.
                    By this token all I have
been taught of
transformation is unlearned still,
                                badly
learned,
          or not well learned
enough

For Wong May

> She who brought me, to New York,
>> from
the Haute Savoie, a bag of
Rosmarin, a bag of Laurier, a jar of
Herbes Aromatiques & one of Chervil Moulu—
I've seen her cutting scallions,
>> paring
vegetables into a great pan on a French stove in
Seyssins, near Grenoble, from which
miraculous dishes emerged:
>> meals
in the colors of Chinese landscape paintings,
>> textures
of Chinese prints, precise in
density
> & the smell of the earth in them,
smell of trees & gardens, mixed
sometimes with the smell of the sea—
the separate smells & textures paired or three'd,
>> savory
& exact in separateness,
> as she is
in her words, no waste in her
& moving in ways most needful only,
>> seeing
with exactitude, with clarity
>> in what the body
needs, what it remarks on,
> knowing

her thought at the root,
                              whose essences
speak one to another,   a texture
of nerves & flesh,   pointed
as stardust: the stuff we are
made of
            (as scallions are made
             of electricity)
                        by the sun's power.

NEW YORK, 1978

13

The Nikē of Samothrace
Louvre (February 16, 1975)
for Stefan

There she is
            (John said
coming round the corner
of the hall
            & we turned to the stairway
          to find her standing
in that wind that charged her
                  in
a forward movement
               (yours in
               your life
                   & to
               the very end in
               the speaking
               of your eyes)
lit up by the air where there is
no quietude,
            no final
compromise
            (no falseness
            of acceptance)
or by water   broken
into light continually,
because the reach is farther
always & ahead,   though
firm in the wind,
               & aware of
danger—
          That wing that rises

14

above her in the fullness
of her courage
                  knows nothing
that cannot be transformed,
                          knows of
no water unstirring

OSSABAW ISLAND, GEORGIA, 1975

15

Duende

        The old woman
with no voice left
            (but able still to
            stand up on the stage where
            the others stood)
whose tone only, whose movement
of the hand & opened mouth, whose eyes
                        widening
on the brink of fury uttered
out of pride those tones,
               letting
them fall in recklessness.
              She knew—
& the accomplished one,
             whose lilts & trills
the audience was cold to:
              all those enticements,
caressings of the voice & arms
             flinging
of shoulders
        were all for nothing,
who in her anger
            could give finally
only her grief.
        They knew her
then
    as Lorca tells it.
           And the gypsy-child
with eyes half-closed & brown fists
clenched, in Calle de la Cruz,
            for whom
the doors & windows of that street were
thrown wide open
        so men & women

stood the length of it   unmoving
                    (silent)
to hear him stamp his small boy's feet
in shoes too large for him
                    once
& again
       & arch his backflung throat
to call upon extremity
(for all of us)
           that noonday,
that street of the hard sun

LONDON, 1971

17

"The World He Has Come To Know"
Collingwood, *Principles of Art*   *for George Oppen*

The voice
of the self
which comes to know
itself
        is in the voices of gulls complaining
in ritual circles:
                flight over the weedy
piers & profiles of long-legged
sea-birds posed in dignified
contemplation,
                standing
against each other in a grouping
of numbers   five   seven   and
three   (the mystical
                a stance that rebukes
the world that is not yet language

                As Verdi's bust can speak to
the pigeon upon it,
                so the river in blankness
of light,
        the steamboat's wake,
                air's coldness
speak—
        the battering clouds, the wateryness
the smell

NEW YORK, 1959

18

La Belle Otero

Being one of those who postponed
her real self so much,
                              letting
others lead me   (or not)
                              being loved
& loving so much,   touching what I could
in the dark,   it is
the life of La Belle Otero
entertains me—a woman who used
her capacities to the full,
                              from
the beginning,
                    with nothing
left over,   nothing left to be
hurt,   whose hardness
in dealing with the world was equal
to the world's hardness itself.
                    To Colette she said:
There's one moment in a man's life, even
if he's a miser,
                    when he opens
his hand wide: the moment
when you twist his wrist!
                    Those muggers
who jumped me the other night, directed
by the whores whose costumes amused me so much,
                              they knew
that trick: twisting
my wrist   so I'd
drop my bag (keys, money, address-book,
                    S.'s photograph in a locket)

They knew it well   & I lacking the hardness
of mind to stay far out of their reach
that night.
                    La Belle Otero
living out her life until 97, with no one
to talk to in those final years,
                              living
without regrets or nostalgia
                              How well she fits
into this world (the world of then)
the world of now, also
                    At her funeral
only the Deauville *croupiers* remembered her
with a wreath
                    And Colette tells us
how she ate 6 portions of oily Spanish stew:
puchero.
          But we remember her
because she danced,
                    danced the *fandango,*
once even on a table at Maxim's,
                              & because kings,
dukes, emperors
                    (such as Nicholas II of Russia
& while his people starved)
                              paid heavily
for her favors: the stocky body
with the tiny waist,   broad hips.
                              We remember that
she made life fit her needs completely—those concrete,
gross, material needs

           & how she lasted
despite the heavy eating, the grossness!
                          & I whose needs
are less consistent, less simple perhaps,   who long for
certain things   but even more for
their evocations,
              for the in-between things
we call less simple—I should have
loved to see her dance.

NEW YORK, 1981

Charles Olson (1910–1970)

"the individuality of the body is that of a flame
rather than of a stone, of a form rather than of
a bit of substance"
>   Norbert Wiener

White light on snow in Gloucester
January the thirteenth   Tuesday
>   from the train
the levels of frozen water
thicken from one crust to twenty
>   Over the mud-flats
along the marshes   a sea-light
windless
>   Frost   ice   snow   curving
>   alive in waves of
>   the sea
shallow after shallow   deeper
>   level after deeper
>   grading
blue   blue-grey   steel-grey powdery
light
>   gulls & herons stalking
>   in the cold still pools
>   narrow-
>   beaked   long-legged

>   After the snowfall
>   a white stirring

>   There is an exchange of all things
>   for fire   of fire for all things
>   The condition of flame is what we
>   aspire to says Heraclitus
>   but cannot hold it

No more the flame does   Blowing
on a knife-edge   fire moves upward
for an instant   dilating
contracts to ashes

The night I heard that you'd died & I
just beginning to see you whole
                              I lit a candle
without knowing why
                              I burned the sandalwood
Wong May had given me
                              The sticks curled
downward crumpling   powdered away
                                        sharpening
the air

Fire in its advance will condemn & judge
                              all things says Heraclitus
That night it was icy   What had been dark
was shorter   the light coming earlier
after the turn of the year

Something went out of kilter
the balance thrown off
                              A plane in space
tilted   A coldness
whistled through its own teeth
                              The big noise
of a new emptiness rushed past us
                              A need to talk to friends
about you   to shelter from the effrontery
of the dark
              turned me

to her   "this woman"   "the self-housed one"
          she of the bold & of the shy eye
          & Kate your daughter
          in the shape of a gypsy swan
That day in Gloucester
                    A day for you Charles
                    It reached where you said it could
                    Gloucester of the cones
                    & of the distances

Under the snow a fire
barely moving
                    the sunlight
                    a sea-vibration

NEW YORK, 1970

"Seldom Is A Gothic Head More Beautiful Than When Broken" *Malraux*
for Emma Raphael

She with the lines covering
her face   as the lines in a stone
or a branch,
                or a stream of water
or sand in the tide
                or a field of grass
in a storm retraces the days the dust the rain, sat
broken with her hands in her lap and her body
bent to one side mourning
                        Death
inside her
            in the balls of her eyes, the roots
of her hair, her heels' balls and her spine
                        She was not here but
there   with sand blown
back from the water
                    inside of twigs'
bark and underside of the dogwood veined
leaf,   ribs of cloud
unshadowing earth's side with
forests,
        each a portent, each line
a wing,   she speaking,
                    each a fleetness
Moving with sides of buildings
                        water running
and streets going crossways into
clarity.   Back from there into belief,
here   into grace.

BLACK MOUNTAIN, 1953

25

Leo Nikolayevich Tolstoy

Who has my father's nose & at twenty-five
the face of my half-brother
                              & whose daughters
have my mother's face,
                              my temples,
my mouth,
              who walked the earth attentive
as he had made it,
                              observing it
with passion & who could not be
denied his truth,
                    for whom when he was
deathly ill the train-wheels
stilled themselves,
                    the engines
were muted,
              of whom the peasant-woman
said to her son: Remember him;
he loved us
              & the railway workers'
banner at his funeral read: for Leo Nikolayevich,
for his love,
              who, over eighty, riding
seven miles, brought back a pocketful
of mushrooms & told his wife: How beautiful
they smell: smell them,
                              which told her
he was well again, who longed to
give his wealth away,
                              who wished to sleep forever
beside the little branch that taught men how to
love,
      who wished to do no wrong,

(my ancestor
         whose body
tuned by riding haying skating
                 could lift a wardrobe
at eighty
      smelled like a cypress tree

NEW YORK, 1970

Provence

Here the sun, violet,
gives us that light Cézanne was
thankful for continually,
                 while at night
we are left alone,
               challenged only
by the frozen moonlight,
                  and the stars
Hilarious in their wheeling violence blow
air from our lungs,
               blood from our bodies,
rock our bellies sick—
               what the stars
in their blazing courses say.
               So he
slept always by nine o'clock and rose with dawning.
               And that light
filled his eyes and hands and therefore
one must be exact, he said.
               What so clearly
time describes on the flesh, in the eyes'
wrinkles, on throats and the backs of hands,
must be rendered again, with time itself wrested away, and
the appalling drop of the soul through space in
gravitation.
               Over again
the earth is beautiful, again and again
and no light dissuades it and everywhere it is
beautiful again and beloved.
               But the mouth cannot praise it.
You must be patient, he said, and humble
before nature.
               And the work, he said,

gives courage.
                 Only the raised tongue clogs.
Helpless, it says: O my love, my friend.

In the evening the mountain reaches for your face.
Those last leaves carry a message,
                            scattered
everywhere. They ask for you
in praise.

              In obstinacy they spin
Till the late cold strikes
                  (light
of the mountain on the brown leaf
                         swung
off the branch in trajectory
on the pane)
               where even
the mountain-pine, bold in its drawing,
is violet
turning brown.

BLACK MOUNTAIN, 1955

Goethe in Italy

That no-no in the air
when the branches cross
horizontally
        after March
had begun to show & the air said: Yes
almost too much, too much Yes
after the long bleak wetness,   reminded
me of Goethe in the garden-house in Weimar,
                    standing
in the doorway while it rained   & his desire
to fix himself,   to be anchored
in the day's doing—
            & what he learned in Rome:
that solidity he had missed, of the form,
                & courage
to be freer—peeling off shell after shell
of himself that was no longer needed,
              to find
the serious without dryness   the ballast
for his whole life—never to be unhappy again.
When he gave up talking to the beloved
            with his
            inner voice
(in the midst of court-business)   he found himself
no longer of the North, anonymous,   but just as
every rock south of Milan seems molded   so he
could walk now, down a street & wave his arms,
or at least one of them,
           knowing again that the truth
                was great
and even the smallest part of it, true.
           And found
himself, alive in a second birth
and grateful to his gods that he could now become

fully a man, the artist—within that order now,
that joy.

                    The forsythia branch
bloomed before late snowfall, lighting up the room:
the red rocking-chair a scarlet apparition.
Icicles hung on the rhododendron buds   young still
in the snow & the bird-voices of spring.

Life in the senses healed him
of the past year's dying.   No ghosts can
frighten him now as they once did—he has seen
                                    the sea.
Everywhere, as in the *Lehrjahre,* he learned.
When he prayed, the gods never failed him, even if
it was only for the brightest moonlight,
                              when he asked
                              for it,
it was there.
                    At twenty-five
he would plunge in the river nightly, walk
under the stars. That was the North:
to find the self obscured by the crowd.
                              But Rome
mother & magnet, gave him
tangibility, wholeness of the thing seen,
                              a quickness
of response & touch: the whole
fiery image of man.
                    So at thirty-eight he no longer
waded in shallows, but knew
he could swim out now   and far.
                    But these omens: A kingbird
flies in a yes-no of richness
falling from the lemon air.

                    What would the Romans
of Goethe's year, the learned in portents, have said
to that?   Or of the towhee
circling over the roof on that grey cloud
greening into a blue evening?

BLACK MOUNTAIN, 1955

Matisse: The Red Studio
for Claire Moore

What is delightful in *The Red*
Studio is that air of suspended
space moving in unbroken
curves with the eye travelling
as Matisse wished it
                    around
and free and in a continual
flight   but at the same time with
an assurance nothing
can shatter
                    What is free here is not
the eye only
                    not space only, but our-
selves swerving & shifting,
                              a sense of gravity
that's root & stumbling-block also
                              There's no one in
the studio & yet each object
is known & lived
                    & every possible
displacement taken care of,
                              each hollow
sudden in the curvature
of space accepted
                    as on this April 22nd
the blackbird's voice disturbs
the rounding of the air
and in that drop we learn the broken

shape,
       the gull's
spurt over the water,
                his slanted
edge of wing
          inside the light
                 complaining

NEW YORK, 1959

Kore
for M.W.

Winter underground,
                         bareness
enclosed: an adopted
place.
        The substitute
kingdom lasts the longest
                          (is a matter
of survival)
            a means to
propitiate the darkness
                    only that:
a series of lessons
in the book of knowledge of
absence
           If you return,
                    Kore,
if you come back to the sunlight,
                              it will be after
you have forgotten
                  when you are emptied
by darkness
            when
there is no more memory
                    when you have
lost your way

NEW YORK, 1969

Linda's Drawing
for Giorgio

Waking, I saw the lemon-yellow
pillow and the mantel
                    and above it Linda's
drawing on the wall:
                    the female
ejaculated arm,
                    the turning
shoulder, fearful and the twist of ribs and
belly
        Inside them
                    the other
woman leaning towards the window,
                                        her legs
curled backwards by a fiercer
power
        squatting and insistent and
behind that torment
and that fever:
                    another female sits
watching and marvelling deeply

NEW YORK, 1960

36

For Louise Varèse

Having seen her
nearly 30 years ago
                    how she
leapt into the traffic,
                    hailing
a cab for all of us—
                    Varèse's "pony"—
to know her later
                    & after
his death,   running deerlike
to the concert-hall,
                    her face jewel-like
a medallion,
                    & 6 years ago
to see it: curved as the face of
a goddess one could bring garlands to—
the enormous eyes,
                    filled-up
with mysteries of light,
                    the contours
of a flower that never dies
                    and now at 90,
                                        regal
with a new pride,
                    magnificence
of a young hawk who has
learned to look long at the sun,
                    unfrightened,
alive with the sun's fierceness,
                    her own
gentleness.

NEW YORK, 1980

The Piano Lesson by Matisse
for Elise Asher

Space—the grey suggesting
depth,
      little distance.
Presentness in which
whatever recedes is
tangible to each atom in my body

I'm confronted with what is there at
every level, at once!
                & whatever
the settled image, diagonally
opposite,
      or two-thirds down precisely,
within the borders of the eye's
attention, is an arresting-
point,
    a place to fasten on,
hang on to,
        to grab with the body's
tentacles,
      there to be
eased of gravity, there lightened:
                  to lodge
between the breastbone & the rib cage
& dwell there.

YADDO, 1974

The Walkers

The view of Central Park from Judy Sherwin's
window: exactly in the proportions
of a painting by Pissarro, Paris, 1897,
                    in that the bodies
of people moving are
just close enough to be familiar
to us   in movement
& in the pace they move at,
                    but abstracted
enough to see the formal beauty
of their gesture   against the trees,
                    darkening
on a late January afternoon,
                    their limbs exposed in
sharpness,
              while the outlines of their figures
are shrouded by their clothing
& misted over by the lights placed on those
                    pathways
covered with snow
                    against the distance.
              The triangle half-surmised
of park (& of the buildings behind it)
lights up   or leaves in dimness partly
what we should focus on: those people walking,
never stopping (as it seems)
                    winding the spiral
of their day intent on errands
                    on a lighted stage
inside ourselves also.

NEW YORK, 1978

For Constance Olson (January 1975)

Roundness of those eyelids,
                    chin's bluntness
in profile,
            the movement
of a Kore still
                (Charles celebrated
                it)
in the white cotton, Mexican
or Greek   you wore for summer,
                            smoothness of
bone & sinew,
                eyes' brownness
warmer than your skin
                    & the thoughtfulness
always of a maiden bringing
offerings on a Greek vase,
                    these & the assenting
voice—spirals of pensiveness:
                    the recognition
of your eyes
            & the child following
in your wake   or hoisted
in your arms are what I remember
of those years
            & of the 4 of us—
                you & Charles
                Stefan & myself
                            I only
am alive.
            What is remembered

piles itself, thread onto thread,
                          fragment
along fragment,
                phrase over phrase,
                sentence,
image joined to each other,
                          delicately
so a breath might topple,
                          a spark of anguish
blast them to ashes,
                the heat my body trembles with
this moment perhaps sufficient
                          in warmth
to shelter them.

NEW YORK, 1975

Poem

                What utters
me is a stranger,
                is another
tongue
        My words take on
direction—
                they turn
away.   I hurtle
in their tracks.
                The masks that hide
them are beaked,
                are hairy,
are painted white—

                They turn away
their faces.

NEW YORK, 1969

Sky

Sky of mid-January,
                    clouds half-grey,
half-illumined—the grey boding
rain,   almost exactly,
(near Estacion del Norte,   where
the workers live)
                    the same spacings of
blue as in that circular mural
we lean our heads back to stare at,
blue behind the railing:
                    we are the people
leaning on it,   resting or trying
to climb further,
                    the anxious faces huddled
together,   looking to each other
for help, for reassurance,
                    we, as they are,
citizens of Purgatory,   sentenced in it
to go round this oval ramp,   following
the banister which can lead nevertheless,
upward to emergence.
                    But it is here our living
faces eddy & flow, gather themselves into groupings,
pairings, threeings,   swerve about,
                    swing back again into
other coagulations,   toss themselves
at what is nearest,   to reach what is
farther away,   question, beckon,   become what
they can be in a thousand transformations.
                    It is here that
we wound & restore ourselves,   becoming
more clearly ourselves,   honed down to

our essences,
                    here, in no other
place,
        neither above us, nor
below,   where all gesturing is
cramped,
          nor where there is only
stillness.

NEW YORK, 1983

The Window, for Matisse, 1942-9

After a long passage
between narrow streets,
                    the other side of
a tunnel,
          an approach through
a lengthening alleyway of trees which
grow darker with the afternoon
                              or
behind a doorway
                  or standing
in a half-darkened room looking
outward through a window-frame,
                              you catch sight of
something the reverse of
what bounds, what rims it,
                          an opening,
an endless landscape,
                      turning
on itself,   unfolding,
                          exposing always
different planes,
                  (another
side)   without fading,
                          with no
repetition,
            reflecting
in strange confidence what seems shadow
also,
      but by that trustfulness
is shown to be instead
                        light from
the farthest stars.
                    Each stalk,
each leaf in the landscape,   with

an assurance that is almost stupid,
                                       revolving
on its stem,   emerges,
a flame in half-darkness,
                           to offer
an unheard-of color: a new violet,
                                    an unimagined
crimson,   unaffected
by what came before   (by whatever happened)
                                  indifferent to
misgiving,   trust or mistrust,
                         even
its own hesitation.
                    As we approach it
in the semi-darkness,   from our distance,
                      twilight falling,
fixing our eyes on that aperture
                          simply
to keep us moving,
               travelling
toward it   in order not to
stick at the point we're at
                 or
to go backwards—
                  & as we hang on it
with our eyes' tendrils,
                   that landscape,
glimpse of garden or sea or receding mountain
is transformed,   changes again & again,
                          each time
we recover it,   flamelike or more shadowy,
more round or pointed,
                    to be bathed in

& made silent.
                  It is the long passageway,
the rimmed window,   the arching housefronts,
                                    the opening
where the street dips & turns
                        that make us silent,
it is the doorway where we lean,
uncertain,
              the dark alleyway where
we can only stumble
                      that make us ready
in our depletion,
                so we are thrown
                (& all our knowledge useless)
into a depth that repeats renewal
                              & the endless
                              that we see
looks back at us & transforms us.

NEW YORK, 1983

47

After the Turner Exhibition

That weight inside the body
must be shifted,
    that terror
of where am I?
    that spasm
of anguish,
   now that S.
is gone irrevocably,
      that:
      Where do I
stand in the world?
     With what
firmness?
    Does it
hold me even
at all?
  All that is
less than shelter leads back into
a homelessness,
     but by
our pride in it becomes protection
for us,
   never
certain entirely,
     never
fixed as such, but rather
comes & goes in
the presence of friends perhaps,
        or in the watching
of birds' finding their food
      or pleasure
in the carved movements of branches,
       or in
our staring at clouds

& lights in the sky arriving
at the same beginnings & endings
      & their reflection
of continuing waves of light
     & as
we see them
in those last watercolors by Turner,
      made of
our breath, our dying,
    the very blood of
our richness.

OSSABAW ISLAND, GEORGIA, 1975

49

Faces of the City

Dance

That hot spring day
             I'm riding downtown
in a taxi
             & see with pleasure
the fake Italian loggias, wreaths & columns
on the old business buildings,
             shields garlanded
with grapes & even a mask or two:
             the neo-classical.
Farther downtown, behind the houses
are little courtyards, vines covering a wall thickly,
green,   full leafage almost
             & what a smell of
damp earth, roots, of coarse stems thickening
out of the rained-on earth in those backyards,
             tightness
unclenching.   So we're in touch now,
these roots with others
             & this moistened soil or
dirt of the city's yards is simply another layer
of what's covering the country,
             the whole continent
& beyond it, in France, in Spain, in Italy,
in England.
             So when I leave the taxi & remember
my bad left leg & hobble
I can smile at it & think
that perhaps this is the hobble-dance performed
by the Kouretes,
the dance to propitiate the Minotaur,
             & I'll find myself in
the labyrinth if I go on
& face the Minotaur
& be delivered from him.

NEW YORK, 1978

Central Park, August

In this greenness,
                  sitting
as we do,
        spread out
on the grass,   with our sandwiches,
our plums,   hardboiled eggs, our
cubes of cheese,
                watching & talking as
the kids go by on bikes, some of them
without hands, upright on pedals, wearing
amazing headgear,   turbans
& curlers in yellows & orange,
reds & pinks,
              procession endless
of marvels,   a kind of
sober delirium: families
skating together
              (a father
teaching his nine-year-old son)
                    or jogging—
no buildings, no pavements
visible,
        earth smelling sweet & tangy
while our talk moves around us, dis-
jointed,
        in eddies,   breaking
off to look, look at
that, at that one,   our voices
half-amused, half envying,
               the world having
changed itself here,
          the sunlight

a concentration of pleasure: the weekend,
                              perfect
weather,
          high-heartedness
more perfect even
than weather.

55

The Vertical

Across Hudson Street & weighted
by shopping bags
            I thought of
weightlessness:
            a half-circle
of gulls pulled in the horizontal
of wind & swaying
gleefully—
            the plumb-lead
of tugboats digging out
space beneath them,
            tearing
the river up in strips behind them
to keep themselves afloat,
            suspended
half-in-the-air, half-out-of-it,
            to stretch
their element
            as I stretch what is
vertical in mine

NEW YORK, 1971

Neither Yes nor No

If along the river,
                    the bushes
bud,
     the trees stick out
excited twigs,
                the blossoms
of the cherry
bleed red upon white
                     & persist in
so doing
          (even with the faintest
perfume)
            the launches
are painted fresh
                  & the gulls still whimper
strangely—a warning threaded
with the distances they need
                             & the weeds
grow hard with bubbles,
                         I must walk
walk there,
             walk & think
of nothing,
             nothing
at all, flatten
my life out
             I can say neither
yes nor no here any longer
(have said no too often)
                         here where so little
helps,
       where
so much injures us

NEW YORK, 1960

The Mulberry Tree

          The dark purple
mulberry tree of my childhood
in the New York Berkshires
in June   is what I remember
               in Central Park now
in the Shakespeare Garden
            with the label
Morus Negris,
        the dark-brown, smooth-barked
little tree,
      leaning forward, alert,
           with tautened
branches curving upward
          & the snow around it
during March still:
        a cutting
of the tree that Shakespeare planted
from the slip that King James gave him
             (so the notice reads:
          to foster
the breeding of silkworms in England)
           the tree he planted
outside the window where he sat writing *The Tempest,*
          and I, for one,
believe it,
      for this is a noble
little tree—I wish it his, Shakespeare's,
           of that
lineage
     & came upon it
for the first time in early autumn,
          the pale yellow
leaves flying up instead of
downward in an unexpected

magic
      & everywhere in the park that day were bridges,
pathways,   streams & stepping-stones
                         remembered
from my childhood games:
                initiation-trials
                (or rites of entrance)
so that morning I was companioned
by a girl of seven or eight (myself
                    who darted
across ponds & streams, surefooted,   but still
frightened & too proud to
show it),
     & this time also flying along those trails,
discovering shortcuts & crisscrossing,
                     observing
pairs of lovers disappearing at the far ends of
bridges,
     feeling (as I had, those earlier years)
inches above ground,
              thinking: *Morus Negris,*
Morus Negris—the name full & heavy on
my lips,
     full & sweet & pointed,
              (like Othello's name,
              the Moor of Venice)
          seeing
the mulberry-tree at New Place, Stratford, in
that quartered garden,
             swans floating
downstream on the Avon,   calmly
past the house where he was sitting,
writing *The Tempest,*
        using

all he knew of ripe, of sweet, of dark enough to
shape a globe of summer
                        & of purple.

NEW YORK, 1977

Central Park, May 1980

23rd of May, temperature nearly 90
giddy with lack of sleep,
                         I'm wandering
through the park,
                    the park of
my childhood,
                  near a bridge that I can
remember (from my 7th or my 8th
year).
            There's Rin-tin-tin, in bronze, the worn metal,
the letters on the pedestal,
                              I remember
it all intensely:
                   this is
where we played at initiation
rituals for a game we'd invented
                                 & the statue figured
as one of the points or landmarks
for the feats that had to be accomplished
& the bridge also
                     & these steps beyond it
& the paths winding in circles
over the lakes,
                 the rocks piled over the water,
the trees & the rustic handrails,
                                  people rowing
in boats, slowly,
in this heat.
                On a bench a boy lies, with his head in
his pretty girl-friend's lap
                              & a man sits fishing
in deep concentration,
                         but doesn't he

have his arm around somebody's
waist?
      Blind we were to the other
people in that park when we were
seven or eight,
            but our traces
are here: those hiding-places,
                those rocks
we leapt from, the Mall, the fountains,
                  the Pagoda
taken over now by these other generations
                    & they link me
to them—to that father
carrying a little girl on
his shoulders
        & to her mother
and to the little girl herself,
              myself.

NEW YORK, 1980

Flower-Seller

Wheeling a cart down Amsterdam
near 70th Street,
                the man calls
out: a dollar a bunch!
                    forsythia, iris,
mimosa, tulips, each a dollar
a bunch
         Where d'you
get them? I asked him.
This morning, down in the
market. The mimosa
will last for weeks—they're dry
                  No, give me
the iris—the eyes of the iris, the eyes of
the face looking down-
wards into the shafted sea, the dark, the purple,
along the Mediterranean,
                  deepest of eyes,
the face of the sea astonishing
me forever.
          I don't forget, as the iris
forgets & remembers
nothing, both at once
              I have no change, said the man, for
he'd sold nothing at all & a minute later
galloped back toward me
down the street: Put them in water!
What did he want with flowers?
                  Faint, faint, the odor
of the iris, & after 36 hours the petals
curling a little,
dry & the fragrance heady & deep,
deeper than any water

NEW YORK, 1976

63

Landscape
for Jonathan Williams

                    Where we sat
the desert disappeared: a moviehouse
a restaurant   a cab   a coffeehouse

Where we talked the earth was broken
A line of green sprang up
and made a shape. The soil

was watered. Where we sat
the sky seethed for a little
while   then opened

cleared   then let
a wind that smelled
of wild herbs growing

on rocks beside the sea

come through

NEW YORK, 1969

West 70th Street 1962

I find it right that
(the world being what it is)
I should live
on a street among those who are shabby
distressed & worn
& not a face
akin to mine around me,
among
strangers truly,
for nearly
five years now,
surrounded
by alien faces.
I find it right so,
in the
world as it is,
that I should know these things
in the flesh
(and deeply).
When I see
the pale Puerto Rican child with the thin face
and wide mouth
patting the white dog
fearfully,
while the big black looks down at her
with concern:
it is
for them too that I write these words today.

NEW YORK, 1962

The Secret

Your yellow, your red, Mondrian—
they're in the square windowpanes
of the Greenwich Avenue gym which I pass, almost
daily.
        On my way to the health-store
& as I walk back toward the river
where the sky is orange,
                    pale orange, fading
into apricot,
           I feel it's a secret
we have between us,
               when I pass those windows,
red & yellow; where nothing
fades into anything
           & nothing blends
           & orange, pale orange
composed of yellow & red
               (as they told me
               so many years ago)
does not exist,
           for red exists alone & complete in
relationship
        to yellow,
absolute yellow.

NEW YORK, 1978

Scorched Earth

Scorched earth
                & I ride up
in the taxicab on Broadway
this morning with a taste of coaldust
drying out my mouth & my insides
blackened—
                But not to miss it,
not to miss anything that happens:
the truck stalling
in weighty importance
                        & the fronts of houses
on the side streets
                        & the young man leaving
the house for the day
                        & looking
about him to see what's up
                        & people
zigzagging between the cars in the traffic
making me gulp for them,
                        even the cold,
the no-sky: to make them
serve, save you,
                give you
your voice back
                with the charred coal,
the glimmer of blackness
in it.

NEW YORK, 1971

New York Subway

The beauty of people in the subway
that evening, Saturday, holding the door for whoever
was slower or
left behind
   (even with
   all that Saturday-night
   excitement)
& the high-school boys from Queens, boasting,
joking together
proudly in their expectations
& power, young frolicsome
bulls,
   & the three office-girls
each strangely beautiful, the Indian
with dark skin & the girl with her haircut
very short & fringed, like Joan
at the stake, the corners
of her mouth laughing
      & the black girl delicate
as a doe, dark-brown in pale-brown clothes
& the tall woman in a long caftan, the other day,
serene & serious & the Puerto Rican
holding the door for more than 3 minutes for
the feeble, crippled, hunched little man who
could not raise his head,
      whose hand I held, to
help him into the subway-car—
        so we were
joined in helping him & someone,
seeing us, gives up his seat,
      learning
from us what we had learned from each other.

NEW YORK, 1979

Courtyard at Night, Bank Street, Westbeth

If there is power flowing
from those stars
                    south of the courtyard
I wish to move with them,
not against them

                    I wish to stand in their
                                        currents.

If the small sickle of the moon hanging
west over the city can cast a light
that reaches as far as I am,
                    I want to
shine back at it
                    & inside it.

If they reach me at all,
                    I do not wish to
be cured of them
                    I wish to tremble with them
I do not want to shake them off—
                    so that
in that stillness I can say later,
(much later)
                    these were the years of
my hope.

NEW YORK, 1971

That Bright Grey Eye

The grey sky, lighter & darker
greys,
            lights between & delicate
            lavenders also
blue-greys in smaller strokes,
                                & swashes
of mauve-grey on the Hudson—
                        openings
of light to the blue oblong
off-center
            where the door to the warehouse
shows—
            the larger smearings darkening
                                    deep
into blues
            So alight that sky,
            late August,
early evening,
            I had to
gasp at it,
            stand there hardly moving
to breathe it,   using
whatever my body gave me,
                        at
that moment   attending to it,
thinking:
            Turner, he should have
seen it,
            he would have given it
back to us,
            not let it die away
                            And that other
evening, walking down Bank Street from marketing,

the sky fiery over the river,
                              luminous but
hot in its flowering also,
                    rich in color
as Venice seen by Guardi—more aflame even,
the sky moving in a pulse,
                        its fire breathing
in a pulse verging on danger—mane of a lioness
affronted.
                That brilliance—the eye of the lion
filled to the lids with
flame
            And his eyes, Turner's, that bright grey eye
at seventy-six,
                "brilliant as
the eye of a child"
                    who grew his thumbnail
in the shape of an eagle's claw,
                                the better
to use it in painting
                    In Kirby Lonsdale, Yorkshire,
where Turner first drew mountain-landscapes,
                    I found Blake's *Marriage
of Heaven and Hell*—sold for two guineas, 1821
& Turner aged 46 that year
                        & there I read:
"And when thou seest
an Eagle, thou seest a portion of genius.
                                Lift up
thy head," says Blake.
                    These afternoons now,
                late in September, 76,
the sky, the river are lit up

at the end of Bank Street, at Bethune.
                              The pavement
trembles with light pouring
upon it
            We are held in it.
We smile.
            I hold my breath to see if
the cashier in the supermarket
will be gentle with the old lady who cannot
read the price-tag on
a loaf of bread.
                  Then I breathe freely,
for yes, she is helpful, yes, she is
kind.
            Outside on
the pavement, the light pouring itself away
is the light in the eagle's
eye   (or the eye of
a child)
                        (I saw it in a man's eye once:
                        but he's dead now more than
                        four years)
Drawing heat out of
surfaces,
                  the light is
without calculation,
                        is a munificence now,
is justified.

To Love is To See
Amare est videre
(Richard of St. Victor)

Kindling
for R.C.

A good omen for today:
                    up
went the fire in my fireplace—
                    logs & kindling
well-dried on a sunny
clear day
            (first time in over
            two years,
            second try in this fireplace
            this October
Up with joy   & the birch boughs
crackling:
            a live creature
in my fireplace:
                all the kindling gathered
painfully in trodden or
untrodden places,
                damp & dry, searched for—
to the very edges of the heart that needed
warming,   gone up with
                the speed of birds alighting
& disappearing,
                so the heart's fire was shaken
into its powers,
                blown open
                & set flying.

THE MACDOWELL COLONY, 1974

The Butter-and-Egg Weed
for Josephine Clare

To discover the butter-and-egg weed
(which I've known since childhood)
has a delicate scent,
                    as I
did today   makes me better
than I was   & I am
proud of it,
             as the kitten
I watched is delighted
to show us whatever
he learned:
             How to walk up
steps, having
practised it all day.
                To learn, if I could,
one completely new thing daily
would make me wiser
                   might give me
the knowledge I sometimes
fail to have at whatever
juncture I need it,
                 might give me the knowledge
I need, or failing that,
                  the knowledge that
I delight in:
            To discover
the butter-and-egg weed is swollen
& puckered & fluted,
                that it is
tapered to pointing
in the most definite places—arrows

of fruitfulness
              with a delicate fragrance—
is still not enough
              There is more to find out
about it,
        more that I
need to learn on another day

YADDO, 1974

Conjuring

Finding the names of birds here,
of flowers, important, I say I must
know them, name them,
                 to be able
to call upon where their magic
resides for me: in naming them
myself—to lay hold upon whatever
quivers inside the bird-calls,
                       the dipping
of tail or wing—
           to know it
inside my hand where power
of that sort lives
             & in my fingers
wakes & becomes
             an act of
language.

THE MACDOWELL COLONY, 1969

The Basket

The basket slipping,
                    apples, onions,
                    a tablecloth sliding
in a torrent,
                    pears tumbling,   a dish about to
take off,
            the table beginning
to glide away,   tea-cloth sprawling,
                              & all the weight of
the world cascading,
                    falling
away to nothing: if we are not there
to hold them.
                    What the Cherokee know of
when they sing & pray to the sun on
the horizon at dawn: to lift it
higher into the sky—that nature is not
"an array of objects simply out there, but
something that must be interpreted
                              that
slips under our gaze"   something "we catch in
the butterfly net of ourselves"   is what
Cézanne knew,   but more precisely,   as
his landscapes buckle, heave, draw themselves up
& would pour away
                    if we were not
there to receive them,
                    taking into
ourselves that shifting, sometimes
torrential flow,   splattering away of
tea-cloths, apples onions.
                    It is we also who are
other than "objects out there" as nature

sees us—those currents inside us,
                              the blindly flowing
stream of functions,   elements
grappling each other which stand in need of
the torrent outside,
                        we who reach for it
outwards, grasping
what we can with tentacles of our eyes, grip of
body—hands, feet, breastbone, circulation
of bloodstream,
                        stretching ourselves to
hold to what is before us,
                              find the fastenings,
hoops of steel,   lock our joinings
to the interstices.
                        We, too, stand there
to be made use of,
                        be molded, shaped, reshaped
again & again as *what is seen.*
                              Nature, or what Cézanne
made of it confronts us
                        & is confronted
by us,
              so we find the use for
bones & liquids, fibres, tissues,
ligaments & lungs,   where each cell corresponds
to what is seen—
                        that distillation
in process always,   never resting
but revealing new depths,
                              surfaces
we could not glimpse before:
                              those essences

Cézanne has lifted
far enough for us to stare at,
                              making possible the world
                                        inside us,
for us to see the world

NEW YORK, JANUARY–APRIL, 1983

Grasshopper

The grasshopper on my knee is waiting.
                              alert,
                              antennae up in a V
                              & wiry
legs curved onto my trousers,
                                        delicate
fan of tail to catch the vibration
of a vibration even,
                                        eyes intense
                                        & huge
in proportion,
                          concentrating:
When is it best to move?

                    The cat knows this, without
thinking & with assurance stalks across
the chopped-off grasses—
                              She lives
alone & happy
                    though the butterflies
she watches invent their dances
in twos only.
                    The grasshopper
waits,
electric with attention
                          Finally
now he knows: Now It's Time.
                                        Move then.
Go.
     Minute claws pressed into his belly
he takes off,
                    fast hopping—
Now.
Now Go.

ROME, 1970

The Untried
for S.K.

There's a bird (vireo or purple finch, perhaps)
          who breaks through
his normal range of liquidness—
a warbling: "Loud, long & rich" the bird-guide says
into something stronger,
            seeming
to crack apart the strings of
feeling,   breaking into
an unused self.
         These last few mornings,
as I walk downhill townwards, I see the boat-masts
swaying in the wind
           gently,   leaning
a little only,   on a clear day, two sailboats
out, skimming the water
             & in the foggier
weather—boats delicately
shrouded.
       If I could
emulate him (purple finch or vireo)
              I would not
be troubled daily, as I am,
          at not knowing
the name of this flower, that blossom,
           I would
make a song instead, not leaning too far into

darkness,
        nor hidden by distance,
                but drawn
past myself into this richness: silk of the water
shining below the honeysuckle,
                boat-lights illuminating
those surfaces,   that sheen: syllables
no one has uttered yet
in an untongued language.

WOODS HOLE, 1976

Schoolgirl

The purply-red petunia in a flower-pot
on the window of a run-down
house in Church Street
                    has its head turned
away from the street
                    & the flower-pot is
too small for it,
                    so the window-sill
seems wrong as well,
                    but the red petunia,
innocent & half-aware,
                    it seems,
of being ungainly, offers us
gaiety in bashfulness:
                    an overgrown
schoolgirl with her face to one side,
smiling:
                    an embarrassment
of pleasure.

LONDON, 1971

The Women of New Guinea

The women of New Guinea stand proudly:
                                        it is
they who cast nets to haul in
the catch;
            it is they also
who perform dances to
ward off the spirits who
might assail them
                        Long-hipped, long-armed
& with necklaces of nuts & coral they dance,
                                with precision
& abandon at once
                    Their fierceness,
the look in their eyes is
an intentness, a concentration
                            They see whatever
they see, dancing;
                    they know what it is
They know with sensuousness
                        They call upon the forces
within them to counter what may be evil
on the outside,
                to link up with
whatever may be good
                        They reach out to
what is kin & kind to them
                                & inwards
to the powers welling up for
their sustenance
                    They draw upon
what the foot knows
of the earth,
            what the arms learn to

understand of air,
                    what their breasts can
touch in the breeze, the light winds,
                              what their fingers
draw down from
the lights in the sky—the clouds & the clarity
                    They are tireless
until it is over. They are given
to the task entirely, whatever it is:
prayer,   struggle,
                    a means to
ensure protection,
                    their strength shining
as their skin shines in the sun,
                              cohering
as the shadow clings to their bones,
making their strength clear.

NEW YORK, 1977

Young Deer

That it looks out at us,
                              from
that thicket, front legs planted
in the dry gold of leaves,
                              ears standing up

alerted into fans of listening to what may be
coming,   eyes huge in
that narrow head, mouth tender.

How that look pierces us, innocent
                              (in a sense)
but not ignorant of hurt, of all
baleful cruelties in the world outside and

inside the autumn forest,
                              how it holds us,
that look so knowing of us,   of
our hurtfulness, of what the deer tells us

is irreparable, never
to be restored, so that his fearfulness
is more than fear,
                              is a knowledge

like that which children seem to show, weeping
for the unredeemable,   shocking us
into guilt. This young deer with his eyes

equal to the eyes of homeless children
                              looking out at us

& knowing the forest, cruelty
of the life there,   glimpsing us only

in these moments,
                 he sees enough not to
forgive,   bounding away,
neck stretched, hind legs bent for

lightness.

NEW YORK, 1983

The Yellow Daisies
for Betty Klavun

Each time I turn this corner,
                              from the kitchen
to the living-room   where
the round table stands,   I am
revived & wonder to myself: What is it?
It's that rankness—the smell coming off
the yellow daisies,   the heaviness their nature
spills round them,
                              the bunched-up
acrid-green stalks in the grass,
                              feathers
of leaves clustered together
coarsely.
          Deeply buried
inside them is the hot sun,
                              a dry field baking
at noonday,
          a round surface
to that earth,
          the soil cracking open
everywhich way, the heat
                              the roots plunging
anyhow: uncaring, resilient,
unembarrassed
                    They make themselves
known, unshy in the crowded glass
                              & with them
all that *goes on, goes on,*
                    alive, unhesitant
stems pushed out there any way,
                              the plain yellow faces
of daisies simply present there—
                    They make no

bones about it:
                    the joy they offer
in their crudity—
                    how that roughness
restores me—
                    nothing
is more nourishing than they.

NEW YORK, 1978

Lesson in the Academy Garden, Rome

The cat all day
from eleven in the morning
to six in the afternoon
                        sits tensely
in one spot watching:
                        a fullness
of attention given
                        to the game it's stalking
                                (a bird, a baby
                                    squirrel)
not swerving for a moment even
after leaves, flowers, bushes
for sniffing,
                renouncing
the usual daily pleasures
                        & offering
his self fully
to this only,
                as I long to offer
myself for a single hour
to what I'm after.

ROME, 1970

92

The Swan

That moment,   the big swan soaring
into the air,
               across the river
when you turned me round, saying:
Hilda, look—& the huge bird pivoted
in the light, lifting its wing, its neck,
bending its body sidewise as it
curved again, downward,   dipping
enormous in an arc of
power,   (a magnificence)
a white stroke doubled,
                    bolt of
white thunder in the watchful air—
                    that time only,
having been with Leda always,   earlier,
                    that time I was in
the double whiteness,
                    with Zeus.

NEW YORK, 1983

Firstly

As the dolphin reacts to music,
                          flicking
his slippery tail & arching
his back,   little Angus
aged eighteen months humps up his back
                          & sways
on his feet,
          so the African delegate
from the Cameroons
                    for the first time
sees snow falling & presses
his nose to the window-pane
                          crying out:
Beautiful!
          How beautiful to see!

NEW YORK, 1958

Darker

Darker

A bed
a bed full of flowers
                    (of love
a garden
Behind it the sea

Which flower becomes
which other
flower   does not
matter
            The flower turns inside
out & becomes an alternate
shape of petals
                    another
color
        & mixing
its smells becomes
                        a mixture
                        (though still a flower)
of smells
            a stronger
smell
        darker
& curving raucous
            into laughter

of the body.

NEW YORK, 1967

Mallorcan Love Song

I know why for a week
I have not slept more than half the night,
awake with the small moon
                         & with every
bird-cry,
        every shift of light:
                   I have
this burden on me which will not let me sleep

I have the sweet
pain, the *douce douleur* the troubadours
speak of
          Ease me
              I am bruised with
the weight of the burden
               Here where they sang,
the *lourd fardeau* is upon me
                Like them, I come to you
saying: you have given me this burden
                   Lift it
with your touch

MALLORCA, 1968

98

For Sappho

      Neither honey nor
the honey-bee, she said
      neither honey...
& I wander with her here
      along rock-cliffs
sides of hills stony as the cliffs of Lesbos
      If for his sake Phaon
she threw herself down into the purple
sea for lack of his love for lack of him
      flung herself headlong
into the darkening water
      I for your sake would live always
even on the edge of those stone pathways
plucking the dry rosemary
      the wild oleander
aware of the sudden
gulf & scrambling
lightly above it
    I wish never to leave the country
of your voice
    I can live here on the merest
grasses
   the half-moist
pebbles
   I can flourish here
and grow stronger
     like this
salamander emerging
into sun for a moment & playing
dead if a stranger passes
      seeming
to scuttle for shelter between the newly
upturned soil & the sheer
rock-faces

MALLORCA, 1967

Siesta

What in that room in
the hot siesta hours was of a sweetness the green
Mediterranean was only partner to,
                           not master—
heavy with blossom as a branch of the almond yet
clear to its depth
                 as an inlet
of that often purple water
that rose too & breathed,
breathed with the sea
                 & had the same
hesitant but finally
unwavering pulse: a beginning of birth,
                        with shadows
of the known-to-be-over-with dead & therefore
a small beginning
rebirth in honor of that which is
not yet,
        may never
be born
        Not to be counted on, but
of a whiteness   moon-white:
                   whiteness
of nails, white breast,
            teeth
against sunburn,
          whiteness
of stone
       Breaking of surf came down
inside that room,
        spray of
a sky smouldered in constellations,
              the Venus

flushed & angry delivering
August
      What would you like?
she asked,
        To know where I am, he said.

NEW YORK, 1958

Air of Noon

                   In the hard air
of noon,
            the light suspended & that thin spray
scattering in suddenness,
                          recurring
slowly & then leaping
above the water,
                   I grow faint
for a moment Aphrodite
                   when I remember you,
your power
            When I am reminded of it
in the white flame of noontime
                          I am struck silent
and I shiver

MALLORCA, 1967

Nevertheless

In that room with you
                    moments
when the soul flies out of
the body
                    through the eyes
                    when
the heart's blood shines
out of your face,   leaps through
your words toward me
                    & the hands that
you call ugly are mine,
                    my hands:
                              they speak
for me
        & those lines under
your eye, your right eye
                    that I noticed
14 months ago (at Benchley's)
                    are a sign of
kinship, the signature
of what-we-might-have together
                    & the air is
with us,   air in the room we float in—
boats in a common sea,
                    moments,
half-hours, maybe, hours, but perhaps only
                    one hour, two
                    & the soul flies back,
you call it back   a bird on a
string   to the prison
of your eyes,   is caught before I can
touch it fully,   hold it
to me
        & the eyes of your soul that had opened

into my eyes & streamed
their light into mine,   meeting me
naked
        are hidden
behind the skin, the toughened
membrane of a bird's eye
                        But how soft
                        that feather is
between my breasts
                (nevertheless
whether you knew of it
                    or wished it,
whether or not you did,
                    whether or not
it fell or was dropped
on purpose
                (nevertheless

NEW YORK, 1982

The Fly

I shall have to pray
to you
        again,
Aphrodite,
stuck again in that same honey-
comb
        as last year: a fly
in flypaper caught
                with my
legs in that sweet
transparency
        unable
to move my wings or my
arms   unable
to turn my head either
to right or to left
                How you have
fixed me in this one
position, goddess, who have served you
faithfully
        all my woman's
years.
        Help me, goddess:
give me the true medicine
for this wound,
                but do not heal me
completely,
                for if you showed me
a way out,
                I would not take it.

MALLORCA, 1968

Neap-Tide

Splayed
under your
gaze
    a starfish
brown from the sea
as sand & my legs up
walking the sky
as I did at five
              your gaze
half-smiling under white lids
hands I had watched
grasping my ankles & coming
from the bottom of the sea
                   passages
of starfish
         underwater
currents waves in
diagonals
        rocking
in the crisscross
of tides
       the magnets
pulling & the deep-sea
gravitation backwards
               reversed & rolling
all (things)
        my arms out-
flung as far as possible & your hands
on mine in the heat
the quiet   the half-darkness
the late afternoon pinned down
                 sun-streaks
sliding on the floor
the sea rising

106

Moon Too Yellow

Moon too yellow for January,
the valley open & too warm
for winter
         as the sun went
leaving the sea
         a blackness
for tomorrow's January
            Beneath the mountains
the ground hard & dry
         with night-noises
in the bushes (where I tossed
         my bag)
            crackling
with dust: an August dryness,
my boot falling on the stiffened
mud,
     my coat on the stubble-
field for us to lie on
          & I
hearing you cry out above me,
               the stars
lit in a sky fed by the moon-blaze,
full moon
        (too yellow by far
        for January)
summer ignorance,
         winter-grasses.

NEW YORK, 1969

107

La Revista

Who walked the width of the room toward me,
that rapid walk in the arc of a
bird's flight
            (two years remembered)
toward me,
            the eyes, the mouth smiling
smiling at me as I smiled & could not stop
smiling,
        a flickering
light & heat playing
over our hands & knees
                    that could not
touch each other in that
gallery of people
                (watching)
but could only smile then
                        blinded
by dazzle   heat
                seeing
the thorny field,
                the Mediterranean
coast   where as we
came together I first heard
your cry.

NEW YORK, 1971

Herbal

Sage, rosemary, thyme—
                    they are
brewed in my tea for healing,
                              mending
also of this quarrel between us
                              They flower
beneath my breasts & push them
outward,   making
a space between,   a hollow
filling itself with odors,
                         fragrances
warming themselves in my skin: a hive weighted
with honey.
              Let me pray to the Maker
of fragrances,   of perfumes,
                              unguents,
scents & sweet-smelling herbs,
pomanders.
              Let us
draw into our breath these tastes of
rosemary, sage & thyme—
                         Let them flower.
They are for warming
beneath the breastbone,
                         spreading their clusters
wide inside that hollow,
                         leaving us
smiling & quiescent.

NEW YORK, 1973

My Dear

Who says,
            My dear, my dear,
& has infallible hands
                    as would have
known for a thousand years
                    what way to
touch me
& with the wisdom
of his mouth
            Who brought me
a red rose that night because I had
said on the telephone:
                    rose-petals,
that's what I want,
                    who comes so close
I thought to have given birth to
that dark-maned head
out of the Mediterranean,
                    who says
when he sees me loving
of him: there & there you are,
                    who wakes
to lean his elbow on the bed,   staring
to make sure I am really there
in the morning

NEW YORK, 1976

Mark of the Tribe

To hold in my hands
                the imprint
of your face, I said—
                to give to
the contours of my language
its charge:
          Mark me.
          I am more deeply
of your tribe than you may know.

          An oasis
          (In Spain, in England,
the path leads down to the beach
          along the sea-wall.

In the wilderness
is where we meet,
          the stars are
fierce in the sky above us: it is
for us to tear away the clouds
that cover them,
          to hold to
the thread that tautens,
that rings between us.
          It rings.
It makes its sound,
          as
does the shape of the sky.
          It vibrates and
no cloud can delude it.
          The air is brilliant.
In the wilderness the stars
are closer,   deeper
to our eyes.
          The earth reels a little.

I can endure this darkness,
                    for what
turns in the desert forces me
into the wind
            & the globe spins
again & again at my feet,
                    throwing me
back to where the stars have
torn their shape in the clouds—

the imprint on my palms is deep.

NEW YORK, 1980

And I in My Bed Again

Last night
              tossed in
my bed
              the sound of the rain turned me
around,
              a leaf
in a dried gully
                   from side to
side,
       the sound of the rain took me
apart,   opened to   what is it?
breath caught in memory of
a deep sweetness
                      that sound
                      unceasing
delicate,   the wetness running
through my body
                   It might be nighttime
                   in a forest hut,
the rain constant
                   in little rivulets
splashing,
              at times uncertain—

safe in each other's arms,
                            the rain sheltering
us   a depth opening
bottomless to a terrible sweetness,
                            the small rain
shaking us in our bed
                      (the terror)
whispering
              End of a season,
              wind from the west

NEW YORK, 1982

Air of the Beach

Wherever I kissed you
                    whatever I did
I'm glad of it
                Wherever I put my mouth
on your body   I'm glad I did
                                Coming
toward me, you came to me
                            surely
gently
                (as the deer come, swimming
                in drifts of cloud
                            but trembling
                with scrupulousness
                                alert
                to the perilous
                            & leaping
                out over suspense
                            on the walls
                of the caves)

Wherever I sank my mouth
                            deeper
than sunlight
                I planted
a sun exploding
                        I rest now in the web of
trails crisscrossing
I left in your body
                    swaying
barely
        (a shower
        of pointed stars)

114

but the heat of it: what I know of
sun's closeness,
                light breaking
the water   at Cala Saona
air of the beach
in whiteness.

NEW YORK, 1969

115

Steps on the Road

The Trail

Cutting across a lawn in Saratoga
diagonally,
        I am dissolved in
smells of cut grass drying & fallen leaves
Clarity & dryness of September
early in the month & sunny
                & I am eight years
old again & trying
a new kind of skip ahead of my mother,
her hair in plaits around her head,
                a flaxen
coronet out of a Russian
film.
    Even she is
relaxed for once & smiling
a bit shyly,
        as if she were
sipping an unfamiliar wine
             or trying
a kind of dance-step
for herself with no one
looking
          (hardly a mirror even)
But I'm ahead of her

It's one of her few vacations
with me: a little town upstate
somewhere in the Adirondacks
after my camp is over
before my school begins
           (later
           than the public schools)
& while she's watching me
        & feeling

like a mother,
            I'm running
ahead   into the country
weather
            (different
            for my birth-month here)
                              & sniffing
the air as dogs do,
                  hurtling
along, as if there were
a trail I had to
follow:
      my life depended
on it.
      Farther
ahead
      the scent was planted
& the trees,
            the road, the end of it,
the woods & where they ended,
                              dragged me
along with them,   & farther,
                        & whatever
there was, I had to see & do it,
                        whatever
it called itself:
            distance?   future?

YADDO, 1972

120

Emma Lake

Late August
            thistledown
in the air,
            the lake-gull
circles grey over the water.
Dragonflies
skid in the sunlight.
The chickadees turn in circles
toward the trees,
evenings.
            Before raining
the clouds make flame-tongues
downward, leaf-shapes,
fire-shapes,
            a stroke of darker
grey dense to one side.
            Enormous
shafts open
in the sky
above the fir-trees in a gold
shining—(a romantic
vision of Salvator Rosa).
            But the lake is stiller
than ever.
            Light refracts in
black and white of crystals.
            The loons skim
smoothly erect and silently
watching.   One dives
below   (the skin of the water
splits)
            returning without

a ripple showing.
        Only the Indians
may still be standing
behind the delicate birches.

PRINCE ALBERT NATIONAL PARK, CANADA, 1964

The Seaweed

As if on Aran,
like those islanders
living on cliffs of shale,
                    rocks naked
as skulls against the wildest
of seas,
        so unwelcoming
that surface—outline of
an island,
            unlikelier
as a root-place than the sea itself
it seems,
            like them I have no more than
a few devices for getting
nourishment,
            like them I have no
choice:
        for vegetable gardens, there is
seaweed   to be
hauled in baskets from the sea's edge—the beaky
sides of precipices,   baskets heavy enough to
curve the back into a
wheel-shape—to turn you
into a wagon;
            there are also
places where the sea-wind   (or the sea itself)
has carried seaweed to be
deposited in cracks inside the island
& it can be dug,   dug out of the rock in handfuls:
one can climb down into those cracks, load a basket
there & heap it high with the blackest
soil,
        no matter how high—the waves dash themselves

123

upon the island, over it,
                    flailing
those rocks & drenching them,
                         soaking
the bare hands that dig the earth up out of
half-hidden places,
                    backs curved into wagon-shapes,
feet trudging beneath those weights of wheels
& wagons,
          eyes washed clean again,
again & again,   made clearer
for searching, for the next deep place
that has somehow been overlooked,
to be filled with earth
                    for planting.

NEW YORK, 1978

124

Cante Jondo
for Barbara & Francis

                        It seems that I am not fit any longer
for the nuances:
                mosses
                        and paleness
of wild roses:
                        I am become now
too crude for these northern
mysteries:
                the wetness,
                        the mist
the rain
        multitudes
of leaves and branches,
                        intermittencies
of grasses.
                        I am impatient
for a singleness, a solitary
thorn-tree,
                        for an edge
of fire
        a boldness
in the sky.
                        It is the harshness
of my desire that I speak with,
                                when I speak with
these castanets
                the hard sound
of my impatience:
                blackness on a whitened
wall, the shadow
                inside the brilliance which they pulse to

THE MACDOWELL COLONY, 1969

Ibiza

What islands risen
remotely out of
loneliness into nowhere
                    and what
rocks
jutting against the sky
                    Southern
scrub-pine and white
fine sand under red cliffs
                    Remote
horizon and stillness
of encircling
bay and waves gentle
yet fierce enough where the tiny
sandpipers rise and circle whirring
in coveys
            They play
assiduously a game of love,
                    The word rises
alone where the purple
joins darkly with the green and the foam breaks
distant
breaks wildly
on the harshest rock-point
with unrecking violence

IBIZA, 1958

Avila

In July, I had loved it—the coolness
on the plateau above the baking plain,
                                    Avila—
but that September, rainy & damp
in the Castilian hills, the Hotel Paris,
skies clouded & swept by wind,
                            cool sunlight
sometimes, an hour or two a day,
                                our room on
the rose-garden, damp always,
                            damp-spots
on walls & ceilings,
                    towels, bed-linen never
quite dry
        (Stefan nevertheless
        working, writing notes on
        music-paper)
                    while I sigh: Why
are we here?
            But then remembering: the walls,
                                    the tops
of them, molded into seats that hugged
our hips and haunches, as if made for them,
                                    shyness
of the shopgirls in their welcoming,
                            their sweetness,
& men in berets strolling
in the arcade,
            bright air of a mountainside
surrounding us
                & under the storks perched on
the battlements, the peasants coming to market,
their eyes wary,
                rooted still in the distances

of the Middle Ages.
                              The town for her,
that saint of Marrano blood,
                              who cried to her
novice nuns "Look only,
                              I ask you
to learn to look!"
                              In that chapel
on the corner of the square they show us
her flute, her little drum & drumsticks,
                              the caretaker
saying   (surely he must have
known her, heard her playing
the flute, the drum)
                              "Era muy allegra!"
"She was a merry one!"
                              smiling
at our surprise.

NEW YORK, 1983

128

Webs
for Muriel

The hand of the unknown
writer on the sand
                    has the message
pricked out in code:
                    minims
on an unprimed canvas,
                         where the ant-trails
tunnel the beach.
                    Serrated
sun-lines in the green water,
                              wind-flutings
in the sand
            make a moving warp
for virgules
of seaweed.
We are caught in the web all of us.

Twice the bird cries out
in the early dawn and is silent,
                                white
the sea-gulls are blown westward
to the lighthouse.
                   No shells here,
but the cloudbank
weights itself to an arrowhead,
                               deliberately,
assembles itself before melting.
                    The sea-spray

likewise, but more quickly.
One bird dashes headlong
eastward.
       The web
grows tighter,
            can strangle:
the limit which our carelessness
is allowed.

MALLORCA, 1967

Helix

Between the first time & the second
time,
　　　stars fell, a tower
　　　spoke
　　　　　guarding our voices,
the sand was cool against my instep.

Between the first time & the second
time　　there were afternoons
A darkening
　　　　　There were clouds
muffled, a weight of
thunder.

Between the second
& the third time
a long underflow
a darkness
　　　　A beginning
submerged
　　　　　& through the windows
the old stars returning
to their places
　　　　　In that fire
a new coldness.

ROME, 1970

131

Observed

That special hell of Dante's into
which we were thrown
(was it
rightly?)
on that particular
street
would be left behind
I thought
But here, too,
behind the darker and the lighter
greens
even among the shadows
striping the well-mown lawns
or above the carefully
molded bushes, its
glance reaches
us, baleful,
or observes in us a possible
field of action.
Even here
where the birds dart hastily
into the branches
here, too,
there is a glaring.

NEW HAMPSHIRE, 1966

132

Desert

That I raged up and down tonight
(you never saw it) forgive. A dry
wind devoured me & could not stop.

The desert dogs howled over the years   drowning
in quicksand, tongues out wrinkling
for a drop, faces shut

against a hail that burned &
pitted. No shield offered but the
blinded head, the lids of nakedness,

the untrained mouth, the cheek that
did not know, the hands
prepared for something else. The window

panes grew steel   grew iron.
Nothing is forgotten. Nothing
can be (and must you go too?

Forgive then.

NEW YORK, 1969

133

Season

You standing always on a
verge—the edge of a cliff   the back road
to the forest whose roots are

tangled, tangling themselves
further, who cannot
be planted,   who may wish for

rebirth   may hope to heal and
be healed   but who end always
knowing no more than

that we kill each other—the wind
drives you also.   The city
has dispersed me and gathered

me back. The city has scattered.
Is there any reason for me   any
reason to remember (remember you

as I do running down the street
from the doorway of the taxi? There is
a fresh wind today. Birds fly

seaward. The dry leaves
this year: I have scarcely
seen them.

NEW YORK, 1969

134

Winter Solstice

A cold night crosses
our path
                The world appears
very large, very
round now   extending
far as the moon does
                        It is from
the moon this cold travels
                    It is
the light of the moon that causes
this night reflecting distance in its own
light so coldly
                        (from one side of
the earth to the other)
                        It is the length of this coldness
It is the long distance
between two points which are
not in a line   now
                            not a
straightness   (however
straight) but a curve only,
silver that is a rock reflecting
                            not metal
but a rock accepting
distance
            (a scream in silence
where between the two
points what touches
is a curve around the world
                    (the dance unmoving).

NEW YORK, 1969

The Cave

November,
            the evening drawing
in,   darkness
                        Tension of joy tightens
in the air.
            Outside little bursts of
laughter & a shriek of
excitement as the ball bounces,
hits the wall beneath my window—
the pressed-in energies of
the twelve, the thirteen-year-olds
                                    breaking
on the air, unmuffled,
                        the certainty
that this evening holds the magic heard of,
                                    read about
in books—
            that it will come
                        (will come! even perhaps
a little later than tonight)
                        That all is pent-up,
richly piled in heaps,
                  to be given
to the others (from me to the others)
sometime, somehow—I remember that—
                                    & how even waiting
just outside the ring of players,
                        the dark falling—
here! outside, here is where it's meant to be—
                              & entering
the house, the hall-passage
blindly, as they do, cheeks the surfaces

of apples,
            their eyes lit up in ripples,
            sparks flying off them, barely
a shadow on them
                  (with the curve of daylight sinking)
it is theirs, theirs,
                  this evening:
the door of the cave swings open.

NEW YORK, 1979

137

The First Abortion
for P.D.

Of the lost babies, I tell you, only
one remains,
                first of the lost ones,
who walked beside me days
on Hampstead Heath (already then, im-
possible)
                whose voice I could
recognize as of me
                        (but not of me)
a belonging,
                but partial,
that one in whose ebullience I could
sometimes rest,
                to think of powers
within whose streams he stood,
                        whose sharing
was a gaiety
beginning,
                an overflow
of April,   with plum-blossom,
                        pear-blossom—
those weeks of the body's fierceness:
a clash,
                a leaping
outward of two enormous
pleasures.

NEW YORK, 1972

Dawn Breaks Through

Dawn breaks through
I cast my lots.
           In the mirror
the dirty face I see is
mine   not mine
                   (ten years ago
is mine.
         The lots
fall.
     The fingers
speak,
       half-weighted.
What way to break,
             what opening into
light?
     that my eyes may dazzle
Let me.
That my face break out of
a mold,
       that illumination
take (me)
        seize
me

NEW YORK, 1970

Presences
for Beverly Bond

The moon brilliant
                (even in New York
last week astounding
me)
     but now especially
urgent with messages,
                    the stars hung about it
in heaviness
         At daytime
the clouds very white in extraordinary
drifts & swashes:
            Calligraphy
of a language we haven't
dared to decipher
           Only attention
               (fullness
renders it back, transparent
         The leaf pitted
as my hand is, smelling
of pine, of moss—
          a drop of the rain
left after forty-eight
hours plops on my moving
fingers holding
these stones, speckled & warming
themselves in the sun.
          The white birch leans in an
arch,
    entrance
to something triumphal
where we should be walking together
weighted by union
        O my presences,
have I forgotten you?

THE MACDOWELL COLONY, 1969

The Puppet-Theater

On the Gianicolo
they saved me: a tide of people
children parents lovers
the balloons the switchback
sidecars & the puppet-show,   the bags of sweets
& peanuts & the women
gathering the first brown leaves of autumn
flatly lying on the grass
& children
running   kicking balls   & smaller children
laughing in the switchback
cars while their parents watched them
proudly & with fear
& children peering
in the empty puppet-theater to see what
could have been there
& below them
Rome spread out beneath the pines,
the outlines
of a stoniness,
a light
an ancientry of hills,
a sister-city
for Jerusalem.

ROME, 1970

141

Carolina Wren
for John Carisi

3 double notes & pause,
                    a speaking
urgency,
            4 double notes,   the same
                              & again another
3 double notes & silence
                    but this time he extends himself
even further
                into 5 double notes
                              & a fullness
of phrasing that crests his wave
                              & leaves us
ripened to expectation for fuller
phrases: a fuller silencing,
                        to a firmer
beckoning,
            a salutation of
certainty   reverting to
the 4   to 3   to 4 & then recovering
his 5
      but stretching us
to the very edge
                  to where the light is
indubitable
            & the air, the space,
                              the morning
have begun to
move unhesitant,
                  my body
before this window
to awake beyond all doubting
into his time
            & into
his beginning.

OSSABAW ISLAND, MARCH, 1975

Coastal

Light heat sea
           all these
in the extreme
                as Pedro Salinas said writing
                long after in New England
all   all are in extremity
                    as we sit
above the Mediterranean & cannot
match it for movement   light
denseness,
            the cries, shouts
                    the laughter
of children splashing,
                the unmitigated
act.
    And along the horizon
edge the line is mauve
                is violet,
a quivering
         of light
              a dazzle
in which I lie poured out
                  refulgent   lost,
dissolved by every season
into summer.

IBIZA, 1961

For Land's End and North

Mysterious, but
accurate is the artist's instinct which
tells you: go *here,* go *there,* not *there,*
                              which tells you
that the sea is what you want,
                                        not
mountains—this light & not
the other & particularly
that sky in a certain season,
                              with what
growing things go with it,
                              whatever kinds of
air, color,   forms of rock,   whatever unlikely
kind of green or shape of hillside,   whatever
voices.
              I wanted them, these voices
here in Cornwall & this sea-wind
along the cliff-walk,   these beaches,
moors with yellow gorse & flowering hawthorn,
these granite walls growing
campion & wild violets on them,
                                        the sky shifting
from faintest apricot these evenings
into colors of pearl,   & in the Down-Along
boats beached in the mud-flats
                                        & children
playing on the piers.
                        I wanted
them & knew I would find myself more free in
this small place
                        than
on any mountainside
or island in the sea
                        or open plain.

CORNWALL, 1980

144

Cape Cod

The pools here,
    sea-inlets
but quieter.
   Each day
a sharper eloquence—
      the familiar
renewed
  & among the rooted trees
       the thickets
of cranberry are a cause for smiling,
how each moment
they seem to lift themselves
slightly higher
   & between them
& the brambly bushes, small inlets
of water,
   holes in the earth's surface,
shine up into the sky
doubling daylight.

WOODS HOLE, 1976

Carbis Bay

Outside my window
the sea–gulls—
Godrevy lighthouse
could be a boat moored in the pale blue-green of
the bay & sea-pines,
shaped by
the winds off the headland,
motionless
in the sun,
purple streaks in
the sea,
almost Balearic
& small clouds
in the sky today.
Why should my landlady then
say: "Go to the Scilly Isles
for sunshine?"
Is it that I'm looking for
warmth, coves sheltered by rocks, tropical flowers
as in the Scilly Isles, they tell me,
am I
to rejoice in the pink colors
of the cherry?
Granite walls with sometimes
the wild hawthorn behind them,
or crude yellow
of gorse,
rocks piled on each other
& signs of burial stones
for those who mattered three thousand years ago
& the sea enfolding cliffs,
circling

headlands,
    these rather.
   When the wind blew wildly on the beach,
        lifting
the foam far out,
     waves & breakers
on the sand in whiteness
after whiteness: foam-surges
not able to rest,
     waves beating
the shingled beach,
      no peacefulness
could gather for more than a moment—
         that hour
was mine,
    that weather
matched me,
     brought you
walking beside me.

ST. IVES, CORNWALL, 1980

Woods Hole, June

Here to be healed,
                    it's possible:
to know oneself clear of
everything,
            needing
no one, man, woman or
child—
            now there are shells, seaweed,
            sea-moss, catnips,
                            sea-mallows,
            smooth pebbles, gulls,
            terns diving,
waves lapping just enough,
                            rising
& letting go,   speaking
of origins—
            a sailboat
dipping on the horizon softly
as eyelids dropping on eyeballs,
                            sun's last stroking
my back & shoulders,
                    wings freshened,
foot, leg, waist & arms
                    happy of themselves
& nothing
divided from me,
                    nothing unspoken.

WOODS HOLE, 1975

December

           If there were a blessing
outside us
           it would be the falling
of the snow
           Evenness
of movement   quiet
of decision
         silence
             A clearness
come,
     a movement
of lightness
           Inside us it grows deeper;
widens

NEW YORK, 1959

Seeds

       Each pomegranate
seed I eat is a step on the road
from Hades
             away from the underworld
             away from him who was once
Apollo and is now no longer
of the bright sun-kingdom
that was beautiful

I bite down hard on my life.

NEW YORK, 1966

150

"Clair Bones"
for Stefan

.

Stefan: His Birthday

When I pick the wild fig in a hollow
watched over by sand-pines
                              surrounded
by the bright green scrub
shadowing the white sand
                       I bring them in my hat
for you
           in the shade of the scrub-pine where the old
boat waits to be mended
                        Over the red rocks
grow the thorn-trees,
                      pronged
forks splayed
                above the extraordinary
sea
    Odysseus came here & thought
this place enchanted because the green
water has a peacock's tail
We come upon it
suddenly in a hump of this barren
island's coastline
where the sand lies pure on the sky and sea: there
is nothing else here
                    Julian Huxley
could have wished to be a heron courting
his mate: rubbing the just-raised
plumes of the other bird again and
again... "to such a pitch of emotion
did it bring them"
                   or like the Crested
Grebe, to dance & dive together
amorously below the water.
                          Neither of these

celebrations of love is mine,
                              human I am less
than these,
              mortal I dream
of you undying:
                    that is why
I offer a hatful of wild figs only
to mark the day

IBIZA, 1959

Stefan's Piece in Two Parts
for Flute & Piano

Above Deyá   in the cold
fire of evening where
                     everything
echoes,
         listens,   echoes
again   and rises
over the shadows,
                     the clear
airs,   angels ride into
fire above Deyá,
                     bells, olive-
groves, mountain-
ridges climb   in a fiery
silence   where the flute
                     the piano-
keys exhort the mountain,
                     the Mediterranean
                     The sea
at all levels
         a reverberation.

DEYÁ, MALLORCA, 1960

Photograph

Look at
the face of death:
                    it is
the beloved's face at
that extraordinary moment
                          we never
watched for
              & those eyelids
imprinted by light only in
the twenty-three years we knew them
have now upon them
an unnameable substance congealing
around the edges
                    The mouth is about to
utter that most relevant statement we always
awaited from it
                    The skin is
rosy & fresh as it ever was
                          We are the only ones who
cannot see that it's altered
                          One moment follows
exactly the same as the next: the sound of
life: then strangeness
                          Everything is
the same as it was.   Everything
is different.

NEW YORK, 1973

156

Japanese Print

You who when I first met you
said: Turn grief around,
                              turn it
into its opposite
against itself,
                reverse it.
                              It is
for you I grieve now,   who are
absent entirely   & enormously
in your absence present
to me,
            present but not always
lost,
            always just beyond reach,   it is
for you I grieve.
                        I sit here
beneath your Japanese
landscape that you carried with you
twenty-seven years: your face pinned up
beside it,   the healthy
one in laughter,
                        then the tormented
face   & wander
in that landscape with you
among the rocks,   the sparsely
twisting curves of bushes,
                                    speckle
of leaf & berry,
                        scatterings
of seed
            & a man with a Japanese
face like yours is caught in
the wind there,   halfway
turning & above him the knotting

of trees,   the opening
mouths of the lopped-off
branches gaping
                    with the unsayable
O,
     the without-utterance,
                         & before him, over
the water, swerving
into the movement
                    forward,
                         in spite of
himself,   his body advancing
on the unfenced bridge,
                         face opposing
the curve of his footsteps, backward
                              feet moving
beyond his wishing or not
in a precision of
onwardness
                    I look for you there in
that landscape of your soul
                         walking
beside you
               & in your wanderings if for a moment
I lose you,
               there are your footprints,
signs of your passage,   your forward
faring.

NEW YORK, 1978

Another Fire

Damp streets
        What was the sun's
light flashes between rainfalls:
                an explosion
of whiteness rising
out of puddles
        (the dark street)
        flashing
of an enormous wing
          Where the moon is
a swan on fire perhaps:
           a white eagle
in reflection,
        & the moon itself surprising
above the city
        whiter
than the sun
        reflecting
in that heat another
fire
    beyond coldness,
beyond freezing
        to me walking
in this darkness
        where I stumble
& recover & in these shadows moving
always toward a possibility
of that burning
        I knew once

in the sweating of your body & the eyes'
brilliance that could never
be quenched I thought
                    & the little suns pouring
out of the fingers
of your hands

NEW YORK, 1972

Litany

               If I walk now
through that room in the museum
filled with a hundred
artifacts in gold
               I know with certainty
that Scythian scabbard
should be yours,
               could match your rareness,
& if I visit the Bird House,
                  as we did together
                  often,
& hear the hoarseness
& the shrillness
               (as you also
               could range from
               parakeets to thrushes,
               toucans, warblers)
you are not lost any
longer,
       but with birds of all weathers
joined & dancing,
               the continents
cawing, whirring North, South, West, East
& whistling together.

NEW YORK, 1974

Cold Spray

Cold spray & the gulls following
in the boat's wake
                              & a covey
of ospreys,   wings held stiffly
& straight, flying
                              as we crossed to the island,
                              the man standing
beside me saying:
                              in Corsica
to this day—the widows
invent lamentations for their husbands,
                                                            as
I should do,
                    who call myself a poet, one of
that ancient practice
who find it possible only to cry out: O, O
who can say only: He's gone
                              (whom that half-stranger
                              in Paris spoke of
                              as most singular,
                              most rare,
                                             tellement
                                             unique
                    hélas)
& she of Burmese birth,
                              slant-eyed, high cheek-boned,
fearless & loving,   royal
in her giving,
                    called him
"beautiful"
                    I am left only
with these words
                    No longer

your eyes speaking
                    Why then did it
come as it
came to us?
               Why did it come
as it did come?
                  & I left now
with the knowledge only that it was,
                                that it
was once (make that believable)
left here now   with no
other sureness

OSSABAW ISLAND, GEORGIA, 1975

After Thanksgiving

The carnations
in the glass bottle
have the smell of spice
                         & I ponder
which one?
            cinnamon
is what I think of
                 (an Indian
                 spice?)
Why then in this weather
do I shrink away,
                so soon after
a springlike Thanksgiving?
                  Why then do I
feel the rim of my heart change into
a narrow bone,
               a whiteness?
What terror
has come upon me
                  again?
Now that you are
gone,
      that I am
alone & remember
my losses,
            that most terrible
one   that turns the beating
on my ribs into a hollowness,
curve of a bone
                 Now in my argument
against myself I try to
prove—that truth is:
is paradox,
            that what is

a contradiction
is real   (a stone, a rock
             to chew on, as he said
                              to cure me,
             that time he burned my tears
             away: a rock to break down into
             sharpnesses,
                            to swallow
             into the reluctant guts,
             to be
dissolved there,   out of
pebbles into dust,
                    dust into
nourishment,
             to learn what I
need to learn to live—

that what is
taken away is given
back again,
          what is
lost
     returns.

NEW YORK, 1973

165

My Hand for You

My hand for you to hold onto
then,
        balancing
you down the stairs,
                it held me
also, it taught me—ignorant—
                    terrors
can be dispelled.
              The mobiles
of the Calder show were there, were there
for us also,
           us leaning
from the top of the stairs,
                the heights that
made you dizzy.
            The hands held on
to each other   They did not
forget, finger by finger
                (the strength at times
                seeming to leave them)
the weighted jewel,   the jewel-heap of eyes, thinking
(to think is to see)   remained.
                We were not
meant for forgetting (not meant to forget a thing)
about each other
          It is written: the *ever,* the *animari,*
what goes on in the characters of your writing.
                Whatever
speaks to move me, it is you who speak it.
          Out of the heart of the earth's body
now, you can disarm me: The sweet earth, Mahler's
particular sweet-smelling one,
              made denser

with you, is possible.
                              No need for tears
No running away—even despair running
away from itself
                              O king, live forever,
I said once (November '48).
                                        The anger.
The torn fingernails. What exorciser
sees them? In our embraces they are
blotted out.
                    We know them,
we forgive them.

NEW YORK, 1979

Stefan—A Last Birthday Poem, August 25, 1971

Man's Life an Allegory—John Keats

It was always music, his brother Willy,
the painter, told me:
                    Don't listen
to him if he tells you
anything else   & it was
everywhere   He can hear it
in the chirrings, outcries,
                              whispers,
syllables of speech of all the living,
the wakeful, drowsy,
                    the unhurried,
the anguished, the unhelped,
                              the callings out,
                              the askings
                              (as once a year the boys
                              & the girls of Ibiza run down
                              the street of the Puerta,
                              arms linked, singing, to
                              honor the island's patron saint
                              the highpoint of the fiesta

                                        before
the exploding stars in the sky,
                    fish
of the heavens descending
in Roman candles,
                    (fireworks of conception)
that too music

        As on a rocking boat in

the Mediterranean night   we are tilted
against the waves
                    but lifted in the other
direction   watching
stars swerving,   horizons
dropping & rising,
                        constellations
in another focus   spinning & changing
pace,
        returning diminished, enlarged, in
speed & slowness,
                    heightened
to make us confront what's there:
                            cessation,
                            seeming
darkness, travail,
hesitation,   the fusing
back,   the question,
the gesture of pain
                    & all possible
joinings,   radiance

THE MACDOWELL COLONY, 1971

Antigua

The yellow bird
flying through the dining-room
feeds on the seeds of the hibiscus
flower & the thin-legged
long-beaked blackbird
they call "sugarbird" here
                           has a polished
head which turns this way
& that
        (but with dignity
in the bushes
                And today I saw
for the first time in
my life the snowy
egret, whiter
than foam,
                whiter
than down, than clouds,
                           tucking in
his head & flying
for his food across the dark-green
field:
        also a messenger
of some note
                O but you
would have wel-
comed them,
                rejoiced in
their presence
                So I see them
& also the hills, the sky, with its baroque
angels, toward evening,
                           the light sometimes
as in Ibiza & I see it, all of it

doubly, doubling for you, your eyes,
                              & see you
striding beside me & the crickets
sing in your ears now
                    more persistently
than in mine

ANTIGUA, 1973

Last Photograph, July 1971

What are they looking at,
those eyes, filled with a radiance
of great spaces?
                What do they see, or
rather, what sees through them?
                         what light
comes out of them from behind you,
                            making
whatever you see there beautiful, to be
lived & gathered, loved,
                  even
in that misery foisted
upon you?
            In what nearness to
clarity did you live,
                that are now
removed to distances whose dark or light I can't
determine
           as I cannot comprehend
death
      & the burden of not comprehending
makes it, your death
              more horrible
& life going on   all the marks of it
that you loved,   all seasons,
incomprehensible also
              & I can't touch you
any more,
         though for three hours when you lay there
dying or dead already—which I don't know—
I pressed my cheek to your cheek & touched your face
with my hands & felt the tenderness of your ears
again & again & the fingers
of your hand closed over mine
                 For weeks

172

after they took you away, the house was filled with
flowers,   a garden—
of iris & lilac & daisies & stock & heather
& red & white roses,
the floor covered with petals
that your spirit might walk among
                                   if it hovered
there in that place—
                    that it might walk there
in joy,
        recognizing the spring.

NEW YORK, 1972-73

The Shutter Clangs

From John Donne's "Goodfriday, Riding Westward"
Meditation upon a Good Friday, ryding from London
towards Exceter, westward

Who rides westward now, as he did,
more than three centuries
ago
    & from where to
where is west?
                Toward
the Atlantic, for him
as for all Europe
                  (the open space!
                  the wildness,)
from Polesworth, Warwickshire, to Exeter
not Wales, it seems   (as scholars
                 thought at first,
                 & Warwickshire not meaning,
                 to him, as it
                 does to us: Shakespeare)
pondering that spectacle of
too much weight for him, whereby
that blood, which is
the seat of the soul, made "durt out of
the dust."
          And there a shutter
drops & divides my mind in two,
                     for I see you
on the floor & the blood darkening
your skull:
          Was it the invisible
you had sight of then?
                (They call it that)

Since your 17th year the visible
was your treasure, focus
of your diamond-eye:
that precision tool
compounded of air & fire—a Venetian
eye,
        eye of your mother's race, Dalmatian.
                O gentle lion,
whose paw in the end was blunted,
                                you shall not
be "left out"   not by devouring
Time itself
            & even now, years after, the memory
of that blood flowing backwards
into your skull is almost
more than can be borne.
                        But I remember your love of
the clear places,   the openings out
and turn again to that ride westward
                        who am drawn backward,
(as Donne was to the East, so I to you) tempted
again to reach you again & again, saying
to myself—absent thee,
absent thee from felicity
a while—
            wherein Donne knows himself divided
from himself,   subject
to foreign motion,
                    as the lesser
of the spheres may be
cut off from the Intelligences,   those that
move them   & so turn into a motion
foreign to themselves

& not their own.
                    So, you who were
in so many ways, my mover,
                         having been taken
into whatever we have no name for,
                         I am left whirling,
often, in a direction that is
not entirely mine
                    & hang back so,
                              as
Donne might do, suspended,
hang from west to east,
                    drawn backwards
again to you & tempted
again to reach you,
                         forbearing always
to do so,   saying: absent thee
yet a while, absent thee
to tell my story.
                    What iron
divides the soul that longs for wholeness
forever & can compass it
only hours at a time?
                    When what is new
as Donne attempted it
rises out of the mist?
                         Is it
too much that interferes:
                         the cryings out
in the street (the manifoldness).
houses, buses, people,
                    the pavements
smeared by garbage,   bruising
of cross-purposes?
                    What clamor

176

& lack of it,   needed
or not can leave our wishes
dangling?
            What use can we
make of terror & our losses,
                        so loss itself may
clarify the eye & make it shine in
unhealedness,
            & what we know of terror
heighten our space,   our leaning
into newness:
            & the eye teach itself
a boldness   out of
what thwarted it?
                        The shutter
lifts.   The mind roams freely,   but
the division is there:
                  where I was
reconciled,
            the unreconciled recurs.
                              But the deaths,
knives plunging
in unforeseeable places—my deaths are
scattered now,
            no longer
weighted as they were,
                  on my breast:
pillars of darkness.
            What was dug there
can be seedbed, and is cared for,
                        cared for,
what was twisted can be touched,
touched,   has settled like seeds now
in my breast,
            those roots that

177

strangled once can shatter
the outer husk.
                        The shutter clatters
& lifts.
            What was hollowness
in me shapes to
an opening.
                    Icicles
that bled my veins thaw:
                            something
edges into green.
                        I am ashamed,
                        ashamed of my unhappiness.

There are no
holy names for us,
                    said Hoelderlin,
in a world that's shrivelled.
                            To call up a blessing
to the world,
                even in lostness,
in grief (the loss unhealed
is what is left us,
                    to uncover
the what is there, the *aletheyia.*

Do you remember, driving,
that early summer, to the Hamptons,   Mercedes
at the wheel—?
                        We stop somewhere for lunch.
Pundy, the eight-year-old, runs into the room,
tears on his face, screaming:
The dog is dead! & I am wet by Pundy's tears
& the dog's body (dogbody) strangled

in his leash
                    & Mercedes
weeping for her son, her dog,
                              for her own living
& dying
          & I cannot see the Hamptons, the country,
                                        the summer
any longer,
             thinking, in-spite-of-it,
you & I will go on together
without end.
              Tonight, the last of August,
                                  weather
changing from cold & rainy
to heaviness & warmth,
                        the moon orange at first,
then paling with light rain   & I walking
through wet grasses,
                      walk also those evenings
the 6 days since your birthday, 3 years ago.
                              How humbly
you took your greetings then,
                          believing still,
as I did, that all might yet
end well for you,
                  the sweeping
curve of your life gather
again & rise
into its fullness.
                  And it was not so.

              There was a little
trail of notes you left to meet me
when I came back from teaching
                        & they said: Be welcomed

to our spaces   my sweet lady
                              & a flower
on the table saying: Flower-woman
                              & a shell more beautiful
than most that said:
                         Listen   Listen
to our own sea
                    (& a little stone marked YOURS
                    to lead me to my room)
                    I am rocked now by the silence
                    These are the stones I have
learned to gnaw upon:
                         I can recover
only what I know—
                         & lean, yearning,
stretching my arms out,
                              still unbelieving
of what is distant.
                         What has rocked me,   rocked me
can now become my prison.
                              But these walls
can speak: I can make them
speak that are speechless.
                              I can hear those banners
rattle in the wind,
as Hoelderlin heard them.
                         I can
sing as we did then, 3 summers ago,
                                   walking
these roads we did then,   singing
the Marseillaise,
                         to help your movements
come back to you,
                         & as

we sang, they came.
                                    Allow me
                                    further.
But those hands that
called up all the elements
are still,
                    that moved once as
the wings of birds do
in flying—
                    those birds you imaged
flying out of your mouth
in thousands
at your death
                    & what were light & fire stretching themselves
ever farther into fire & light
                                    danced with them,
shaping & forming them—
                                    dispersed, dissolved,
made still.
                    Gestures
I never used come to me
now: fists clenching, chest raised in
a stiffness to stop the weeping,
                                    teeth grinding
the sound back
                    & I learn thereby
the in-spite-of,
                    the in-spite-ofness,
of your life,
                    the "premonitions
of good things to come" the year before your illness
showed itself,
                    the premonitions
I must now make true: that greeting, 1961,
                                    from London,

181

of "an unwearing life"
                         & "I salute you
on a clear day...wishing you
a *coeur très fort, très fort,*
                         wishing you
a clear day."
                    The names you gave (Hoelderlin's
holy names): the "evergreen"
                              (image that H.D. sent &
                              Frieda Lawrence)
the "cleanness...without stains" & for
yourself: "everness."
                         Let the stones that
I feed on bleed,
                    let their wounds show, let them
show red,
              Let the redness
turn to flowers—tulips, roses, crimson
carnations that you loved, the Bird of Paradise
your students brought you, as it
resembled you,
                    let them
begin another summer in me.

                              Birds in astonishment
                              discovering
warmth in the sun this morning—
                              from them
flows back to us a mildness.
                              Even
today the scent of honeysuckle
on a bank brought you
alive to me.
                    Your voice & your step were with me

in the dark, with the light from the boats shining
on the silky water
                              & the voice, furious,
of a thrush this morning,
                                        insisting
on his presence in the world
                                        (as we all must do,
                                        you taught me)
& in that spray of notes flung out of
his small body
                              you exulted with him.

                              Can I ride away
from where you   dying
are,
        as I lie dying with you,
                                        you of "the clear sky"
                                                  in whom
no anger lived,
                        whose fire
                        was gaiety   & "the coeur très fort
                                        TRÈS FORT"
Unlike you, I have held to bitterness: each inch of
death encroaching
opened swamps at my feet.
                                        You of
the "clair bones,"   the uttermost
tip of the tree,
                              from your eyes I gather
flakes of light warmer
than any stars
                        in these years that have blinded me.

                        The shutter clatters,

clangs & lifts
         & I move forward
my roots in darkness still —
               but
riding westward,
         even as I'm pulled backward
where you lay,   pulled eastward
where the light grows strong enough to
point me away from the pain repeated, overknown,
to Land's End   to the open water,
unknown
         & riding westward.

NEW YORK, WOODS HOLE, THE MACDOWELL COLONY, 1975-1976, 1980

Beginning Again

The Postcard

That postcard over the night-table,
I thought, just now—it would
finish me,   for it tells me

what is over is completely & truly gone—
those summers of joy we lived in,
the steps we climbed, down to the water

for swimming—completely gone for us—
over—that light that was then
wholly of the present,   wholly,

completely known to us, ours—is
no longer there for us & your voice then, even
at its most tentative, drew its timbre

out of our center, yours & mine, centers
of living, joined there, as two wheels in
Ptolemy's epicycles are linked "together,"

"together"—your word for us
to the very end.   *Reality,*
that word the Spaniards love ("in reality"

they say) it was there, along
those walls in Ibiza that show in the postcard—
that I knew it then, inside & outside,

tangibly, making flesh & bone out of
what we breathed, out of dry earth
underfoot, hot sun, movement of water speaking

our words before we knew them, sky without any
cloud, heavy-grained bread, fresh figs
sticky in our hands, cheese, mussels eaten

at that kiosk on the port, with wine
held in our mouths   (for that we had waited
on streets in the greyness of cities)

& the earliest light of evening   Our feet & hands
lips & bellies grown there out of
the roadside with the cypress, the olive-trees.

How dense it became inside, how knotted
in webs of roots tying all that we needed
together, how certain we were

it was meant to go on, far on, certain of
decades at least, unshrinking, armed against
wounding, stronger than

mutability, befriended by
hostile time.

                You who said: Never
give in.   Remember.

Never give up.   As you
never did.   Never.
When the evening light became crystal

& that earlier greyness was answered
we knew it as "forever"—from "remembering"
to the tangible: steps leading

down to the water, your voice using
Spanish phrases, hot sun, the summer,
the light, dry earth, the sea

speaking our words,   the mussels,
the bread, the cheese, the olive-trees,
the cypress, a sky without clouds & our neighbor,

the French girl playing Beethoven records—all that
"unchanging." That trap we lay
for ourselves—"memory" they call it—

turn it away from those shadows, making it
move beneath us,   make it
the road walking under us,   the sky

flying over & on the most distant horizon
let it change as the sea changes, remaining
itself, but new for us

food for a time of scarcity, reaching
to the unexpected. Send us away
& out from it,   farther

than we could have known it,
shake the dark of it off us,   away
from our feet, turn it

around—not only root
now,   but seed for us
hulled & stripped off & shining,

the imagination a winnowing-fan,
a *liknos,*   the kernel of memory
beaten & scraped inside it,

tossed & flayed until bursting

NEW YORK, 1980-81

Hanukkah

This season for us, the Jews—
a season of candles,
                              one more
on the seven-branched candlestick for
the seven days of the week,
                              but let it be seven
in the sense of luck in dice,
                              seven of the stars in
the constellations:
                              Orion, Aldebaran in the sky
                                                  lively
over Jerusalem
                    Let the fuel
last the besieged   such as we are,
                              to nourish
us.
      Let the oil continue
for heat, for illumination,
                              flame crouching
in the lamp,
                    the glass smoky
                              (December upon us)
the light not fail.
                    The air has been mild
for days—
            & the 7 rings through my life
despite the 8 of this week—
                              bushes
in the doorway of 7 Charles where I lived, 51,
crackle with dryness,
                    are bare still.
That house with the lucky
number brought me luck & misluck, both,
                              like the other

190

that added to 7, out of 4 & 3,
                              that seven
underlying the eight of this week,
the 8 just over, the 7 just under
a third of the years with Stefan:
                              I praise them
both today—
                  the lasting oil
in the seven-branched candlestick:
                              absence
of all fear—the smallest
drop of fuel enough to leap from.

NEW YORK, 1973

Louse Point, August 1978

O beneficence   of distance,
silence,   grey-blue
                    stretching
of emptiness,
               a wideness
saying:
          it is
not so terrible,
                    nothing
is,   nothing
is awful
          in the banked, the blue-grey
sky & the space that is
not only there to include, contain,
                              but embraces,
embraces us all
               & gently,
tenderly almost,
               but with a tempering
gesture: a dryness,
                    a never-
too-much
          So to sit gazing
at the sea,   the mild sun,
                         curve of the headland
to the left   & waves lapping
not loudly   (their weights concealed)
               to sit there
becoming part of the beach,
                         (half-empty)
          a little livelier
than a pile of seaweed,
                    a pattern
of pebbles   without needing
to strain at being   (anything)

SPRINGS, LONG ISLAND, 1979

The Playing-Cards

                    Everything
you have said,
           everything you may have
meant
     & not quite said—all that
& much more that I only
guess at, surmise
            I take into
myself   (& yeasay)
& remember
         & that I could be
so careless,   unknowing,
                   seemingly
not knowing of what we know,
                  whatever
we do not & what we have not
mentioned
       astonishes me,
       shows me
the power of words   (again)
chosen   like that
haphazardly   & now so apart from
what I meant—
           I lay them out
in amazement,
         wonder,
& rethink it
all again
        (But they are like cards,
like playing-cards, not used for
building houses,
            not meant for
structuring,
       tossed out on

waving grasses that tilt them
a little too far this way,
                    or too much
that)
      my carelessness then
like the wind's, the unknowing
movement of air,
                    tossed out
too blindly
            Such weight in them
I had not realized.
                    It was in some way
otherwise
            (& not meant so)

Clear the ground of them.

NEW YORK, JANUARY, 1953

194

Leaves

The taxi takes me through the park—November—
slopes of it filled with the different stages
of autumn:
        on the trees some leaves are gold, some
        russet,   some pale yellow,
others clear brown—a few amazingly
green still,
        while the trees completely denuded
of leaves,   naked & grey
against warmer colors, are
shapes of skeletons—
each bone a moulded carving,
             but shining,
grey into silver.
        Hayden said: Why doesn't she
write about ageing?
        But it's not so simple:
        in the midst of ageing
I come upon this greenness
fresh as it ever was,
        with the browns
there are fiery reds also,
        russet colors
warmer than any I knew before
        & the yellows
more blithe—they smile in
transparency.
        But the bone,
the bone, grey-silver,
        that
emerges—I know it well (dear Hayden)
        & what there is in it
that frightens us—
        but I'm given

more than the grey bone (the skeleton):
>   above it
leaves grow red
>   & under it
the leaves are pure in yellowness
& some are purply-dark.
>   The greenness
is startling, undefeatable—has not
deserted us,
>   is ours still
& of our time as much as any
dark-brown, grey
or yellow.

NEW YORK, 1982

Striking a Match

A match flaring on a rough surface
because in extremity we need them
both: the light, the heat—& cannot
survive without them,
                            so poetry
is written in New York
                            in that clangor
of a million incongruities, points of
juxtaposition,   tension of
silence,   so dense we cannot breathe in it
except at moments
                            if the wind catches us,
whirls us along the sidewalk, clutching
at walls in blasts from the river,
if for a moment we lean back in a chair
in a restaurant looking out at
the street,   or stand with a friend, or
with friends smiling at a street-corner
watching the moon droop over us,   irresolute,
or watch from the window
                            a moment after
we see the first bird that day
speeding westward
                            & know it has
left everything behind it

NEW YORK, 1981

197

The Illness

Whatever germ in the air dug into me
that day must have found a division
in me
      to enter into—
a crack opening into a gulf down which
I slid:
      that grey blowy day with
signs of rain impending
           & in the bookstore
on Madison   the reason
for that split:
      reading the memoirs of Pound's daughter,
              Mary,
on her father—this apparently sweet blonde woman
with a most civilized face,
      not able,
she said, to understand why Pound should speak of
remorse, toward the end of his life,
         nor to see
"why racial purity should not be maintained,"
       & I, fascinated
by that lovely face
      & by the precepts
of civilized behavior taught her
by Pound, her father, as she quotes them,
      & she finding
no reason thereby for remorse,
      saw only
the dead, piled, heaped together
with the living dead,
      leaning on each other,
helpless,
      at Auschwitz & Maidanek.

NEW YORK, 1979

198

Four Days

Ahead of me, in the hot hallway, July,
at Westbeth,
        I see a tall woman
walking carefully,
           & as I pass her
I see that there's a sling around her neck
           & in it
a small creature, pink & folded
inwards,   eyes & mouth shut tightly
against the world.
          "How old?" I ask,
"Let me think—four days!" the woman says.
         Turned in
to itself, the baby nurses
its own body & ripens
until it is ready,
          ready
for the world,
         that world I've heard of
today, in which they speak of nuclear warheads
           & fortunes
foundèd on drugs & gun-running:
            the money
"laundered" through the I.C.F. (the International
Children's Fund)
         Immaculate,
contained in itself, the baby dozes,
deep in its own essence,
         from which there flows,
unreasonably,
      a balm,
        a reassurance.

NEW YORK, 1979

El Salvador

The vultures fly low in El Salvador
                              screaming
at times,
          searching
in the gulfs & valleys
                    on the steep hillsides
thick with underbrush
                    & hills rolling behind them
                    seeking
the dead bodies dumped out of army-trucks,
the *campesinos,* hundreds,
                              thousands,
young men & women,
                    the very old,
the very young,
                    whoever might be witness,
protesting.
          They know where
to look: they have seen them—
what they are looking for,
                    what they need to
eat, pick the flesh off.
                    I saw vultures once
or what the guidebooks called "eagles" but
others who knew & lived there
                    called them
vultures, in the gulf behind Delphi,
                    between
those mountains looking
to the sea,
          nearly 20 years ago
          I saw them,
soaring & wheeling,
                    holding still,

dipping in the wind & gliding,
plunging with it
                    & we were
nearly level with the mountains opposite
in a room carved out of the cliff-rock
                                        & the boy
                                        saluted us
                                        as Achilles' page
                                        might have done,
                                        Mt. Olympus
                                        in the distance
where the vultures wheeled, the mountains
were close as my hand—the air clear, transparent
as the water scrubbing the white stones
at Castalia.
                            Those who called them
"eagles" said they came from Zeus
                            & where they plunged
the valley was dark with secrets.
On the slope behind us
the priestess once had conjured the sacred python
out of his hole to answer riddles,
                            to speak of
what was to come.
                    But who speaks now
in El Salvador where the questions, voices
shriek, scatter,
                    are lost in
the thickly covered hills?
                            In the sacred places
the streams, the mountain-torrents
are transparent.
                    The questions

wheel in the air,
                        they dip & plunge
& seem to separate
& come together.

NEW YORK, 1982

Postcard from the Isle of Aran

You speak of faith—
                    that
I have it.
            I said: an ark to
            ride out the storms
            to come,
                        even
to the final spark.

                    But it is here
faith is:
            this kettle
having grown new purposes—
the fierce green leaves & stalks
growing out of it,
                        fresh-scarlet
of the newly-painted window-frame
it stands in,
                snow-brilliance
of the whitewashed wall.

SHANNON, OCTOBER, 1982

That Mountain

Wer, wenn ich schriee,
　　　　　　　hörte mich denn
aus der Engel Ordnungen
　　　　　　　　　you would cry out
suddenly—your favorite lines in Rilke
　　　　　　　Who, when I cry out
hears me (in the angelic orders)
　　　　　　　　& I find myself now
in aloneness　　crying
that phrase aloud:　　*Wer, wenn ich schriee—*
who hears me
then, when I cry aloud
　　　　　　　　& it would seem
there's no one, you're not there
　　　　　　　　　　& no one like you
is possible, in this life
　　　　　　　But sometimes
this one or that one
does hear me
　　　　　There are
extraordinary letters: a woman writes me
out of the forest, speaking of
birds, of water, of wind,
the sky, the insects,
　　　　　　　　of her children,
her letters full of love for my poems
whose words she knows by heart
　　　　　　　　　& for me the poet,
living alone, a woman,
after a love that built & nourished her,
after a death—
　　　　　　how she sees me
in the grey, multitudinous city—
& would like "to spoil me":
　　　　　　　　in this Purgatory,

glimpses of heaven.
                       & I am grateful
for the young taxi-driver from
Tashkent whose face lit up
my morning—to whom I could say
what I had learned as a child at home: "*Sûo*
choroshovo"
               & to the woman
in the supermarket who stopped in her shopping
to help me put back packets of tea
that had rolled to the floor
                      & for her laughter,
her good temper.
                  It is "the others" who offer
glimpses of Paradise.
                 That night
I dreamed of lustrous, long-stemmed flowers,
formed in the shape of a goblet,
                   one yellow
verging on orange,
           streaked
with gold,
        the other rosy
deepening to violet
              & in another dream
that night my face was washed
in dew,   my body
girdled with a reed
             & I set forth again
as I was taught to do
          to climb
that mountain.

NEW YORK, 1981

The Tailor

Not the way the tailor
sewed back the button
on my winter-coat
                as I stood there
                & tightened
the one hanging loose below it,
as the shoemaker in my childhood would sew back
a buckle & fasten a heel where
the nails were half-out,
                    not in that way—
but something you did from the very beginning
put a stitch through a rent
in my life,
          made me notice
where the fabric had loosened,
                      where
threads were frayed or undone,
                      something
you said or looked, as you listened,
                showed me
a seam was askew
                It was your readiness
to put words to it,   to listen,
                    to move with a certainty
in my underground
                & overhead—
& with what ease—stepping between them
on the path there as you made it,
it was the aliveness of knowing
                    by speech   (touch
                          smell)
by seeing—
          Yet it was in those moments
standing at the tailor's,   watching him

choose only that size of needle, exactly
that strength of thread,   that color
only & no other,
                    his absorption
in what he was doing
                    that I guessed at the rightness
of your choices,
                slowness or speed
of your words,
                rhythm
of your speaking,
                reasons for
what was said
                & what was not said.

Mont Ste. Victoire
Cézanne
for A. H.

Because I can't talk to you or
see you,
         or put my hand on your arm
this morning,
              I'm writing you this note instead
looking at the Cézanne reproduction: Mont Ste. Victoire,
1904-1906—the one we both have—which
you may be staring at, this moment.
                         It is a kind of
ascension of the soul
              (No matter what
                the art-critics
say)
    from the darkest roots of
its beginnings, where the first apprehensions
are: huddled
in indistinctness,   (half-petrified
by fear of what lies beyond).
                     But it moves outward
& to the upper reaches of that landscape
where it finds comfort in clumps of
sunlight,   the golden heaving
of bushes & trees & fields
                 where happiness
is solid as a basket of fruits,
              their ripeness
never toppling into decay   & holding
the sun forever.
            Yet there are no false forevers
here:
     This is only

the middle level & there is no rest here.
                                        All is
in movement, flickering, restless,
                            darting
into farther spaces,
                      pressing
away from the root.
                        But it is not enough to
be in the middle of things
                            & for you, especially
(if you are looking at it now)
                                not enough to
spread limbs in sunlight,
                          warm yourself in
oranges & yellows,   deep golds of
earth,   store your heat
densely in folds & ridges of red clay, sand,
packed soil,
            for you especially
not enough,   even among those
fiery crystals.
                Your direction is
farther: it is the mountain
that you aspire to,
                    it is
that other plane,
                  that hardness changing
into something else—
                      earth & rock becoming
clouds, it might be,
                    tangible
yet floating,
              tumultuous

in metamorphosis: an ocean
                              transparent
at every level
              & visible
to its farthest depths—
                        a multi-radiance
of air, of sky, of sea.

NEW YORK, 1983

Second Spring

The cyclamen,   Seferis speaks of it
often
        (over & over)   it consoles him
for the burden of the ruins
                How well I know it—that flower
of the genus *primula*—I knew it
purple on the pale-gold limestone,
                                after
the September rains—second spring on
the Mediterranean—the burnt summer ending,
                        a self-assured,

a trustful flower,
                hopeful, I thought it,
on the rockface,   near
the thrust of the olive-root,   or the bare bones
of the fig-tree, branches
unlit by leaves still,
                the Hebrew name for
the flower: *rakéfet*—breathing
of airiness, of flight,   of wings beating
upward,
        a delicacy
so confident, it seemed
invulnerable,   protecting
everything,
        so even
the donkey there had need of it to utter
with such hoarseness
his inconsolable grief.

NEW YORK, 1983

The Last Rehearsal

Where something is being made is
where joy is,
    where something
begins—
   the bare bones
before flesh has covered it
      or the innards
of the body where things begin to
work,
   where the cell begins
to stretch itself, the nucleus
to multiply.
     It is a scaffolding,
but one that trembles,
       must be
delicately treated,
      everything around it
must be hushed, listening.
      There the essential,
the bud of joy begins
to move, to shudder,
     to give birth to
more,
   tendril upon tendril,
   to climb outward
over its beginning,
      breath
after breath,
    lick after lick of
warmth pressing outward
       We are
behind the scenes,
    the curtain

has not risen
              They are trying out
the piano, looking at
the lists of what must be done.
                         Here is a schoolgirl
coming now, bringing a cup of coffee.
                    The singer
is trying out her voice.
                Without being told to
do so, we have fallen silent.
               It is
the run-through,   the beginning
of the last rehearsal.
              The scaffolding
sways now with our breathing:
the warmth of it.
             Before the entrails
are covered,   the inner organs
hidden,
      the bare bones
made invisible

NEW YORK, 1981

Winner of the Capricorn Award for 1983

The Capricorn Award is sponsored by The Writer's Voice of the West Side YMCA in New York City and is given annually to a poet over forty in belated recognition of excellence.

Judge for 1983: Stanley Kunitz